Workbook
BUSINESS COMMUNICATION

Third Edition

CASE PROBLEMS AND ACTIVITIES
BUSINESS COMMUNICATION

JULES HARCOURT
Murray State University

A. C. "BUDDY" KRIZAN
Murray State University

PATRICIA MERRIER
University of Minnesota, Duluth

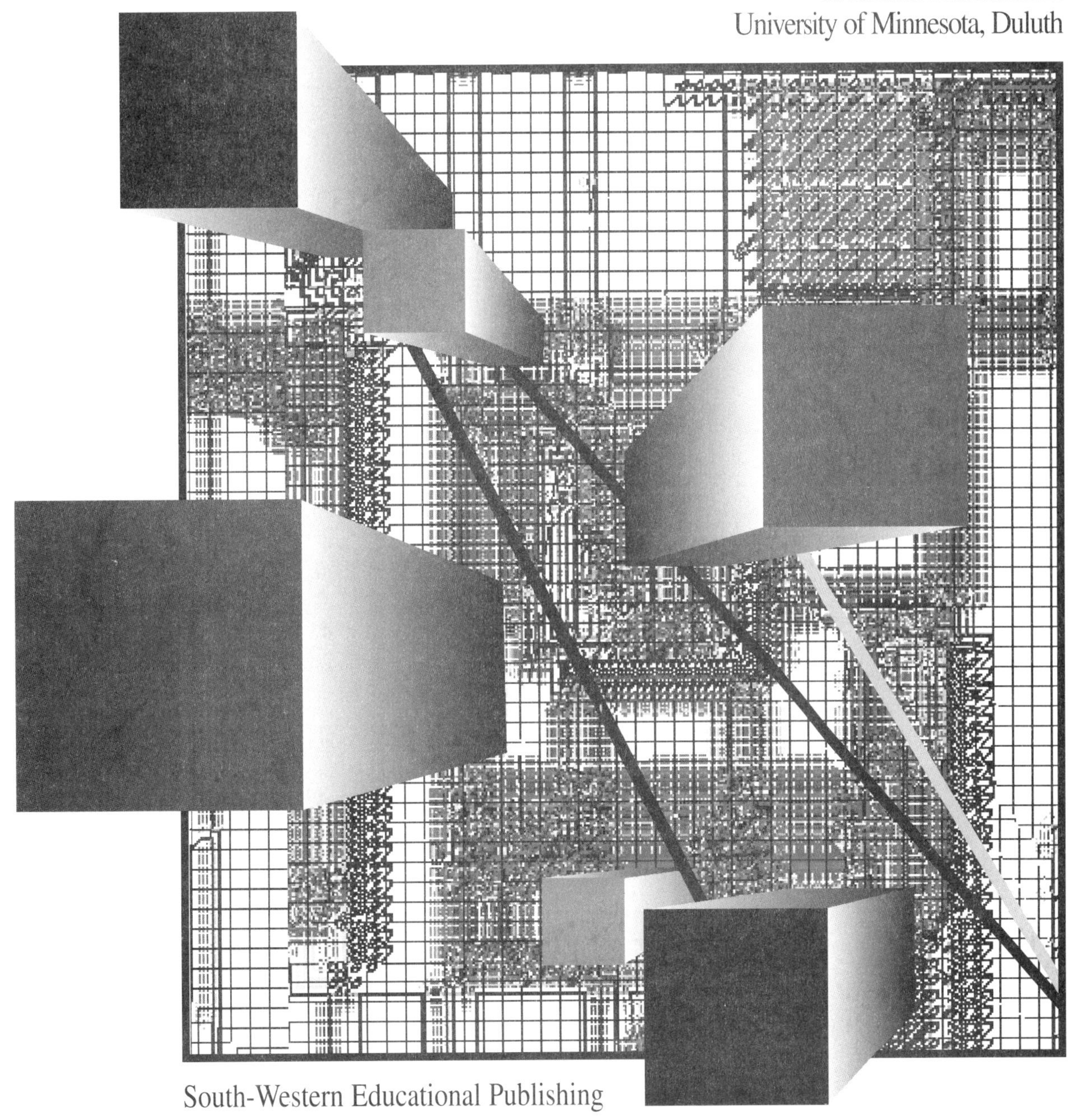

South-Western Educational Publishing

CONTENTS

PART ONE   COMMUNICATION FUNDAMENTALS

Chapter 1	Business Communication Foundations	1
Chapter 2	Principles of Business Communication	7
Chapter 3	Developing Business Messages	15
Chapter 4	Communication Technologies and Techniques	21
Chapter 5	International and Cross-Cultural Business Communication	27

PART TWO   BUSINESS ENGLISH

Chapter 6	Parts of Speech	33
Chapter 7	Sentence Structure	39
Chapter 8	Punctuation	47
Chapter 9	Style	55

PART THREE   CORRESPONDENCE APPLICATIONS

Chapter 10	Formats of Letters and Memos	63
Chapter 11	Positive and Neutral Messages	69
Chapter 12	Negative Messages	77
Chapter 13	Persuasive Messages	85
Chapter 14	Goodwill Messages	93

PART FOUR   WRITTEN REPORT APPLICATIONS

Chapter 15	Business Studies and Proposals	101
Chapter 16	Report Preparation	109
Chapter 17	Graphic Aids	115

PART FIVE   ORAL AND NONVERBAL COMMUNICATION APPLICATIONS

Chapter 18	Listening and Nonverbal Messages	121
Chapter 19	Oral Communication Essentials	125
Chapter 20	Oral Communication Applications	131

PART SIX   EMPLOYMENT COMMUNICATION

Chapter 21   The Job Search and Resume 137
Chapter 22   Employment Communication and Interviewing 143

CHAPTER 1

Business Communication Foundations

LEARNING ACTIVITIES

True or False?

Circle T if the statement is true; circle F if the statement is false.

T   F   **1.** The ability to communicate effectively is the most important skill you can develop.

T   F   **2.** Business communication includes all contacts among individuals both inside and outside organizations—formal as well as informal.

T   F   **3.** The most important goal in business communication is for the organization to gain goodwill.

T   F   **4.** The sender is responsible for the achievement of the four business communication goals.

T   F   **5.** There are three basic patterns of business communication—upward, downward, and horizontal.

T   F   **6.** Informal communication can be work related.

T   F   **7.** The sender's most important role in any communication situation is to analyze the receiver for the you–viewpoint.

T   F   **8.** Using face-to-face oral communication will assure accuracy in serial communication.

T   F   **9.** Detailed job instructions can best be communicated by using an oral message.

T   F   **10.** The sender has a responsibility to help receivers overcome any physical or mental disabilities they may have that cause communication barriers.

Multiple Choice

Write the letter that represents the best answer in the blank at the left.

__________ **1.** Business communication can be defined as
   a. the transmission of data in the business environment.
   b. the transmission of information.
   c. the transmission of information in the business environment.
   d. all contacts inside an organization.

__________ **2.** The most important business communication goal is that
   a. the receiver understands the message as the sender intended.
   b. the receiver provides the necessary response to the sender.
   c. the sender and the receiver maintain a favorable relationship.
   d. the sender's organization gains goodwill.

__________ **3.** In networking communication flows
   a. upward.
   b. downward.
   c. horizontally.
   d. diagonally.

__________ **4.** The most effective words for a sender to use in a business message are
   a. technical words.
   b. words that challenge the receiver.
   c. words that are in the receiver's vocabulary.
   d. words that are below the receiver's reading level.

__________ **5.** Formal communication in an organization
   a. is not planned by the organization.
   b. flows in all directions.
   c. is essential for effective personal relationships.
   d. is not essential for the operation of a business.

__________ **6.** While the use of proper grammar in messages is important, it will not
   a. help maintain sender credibility.
   b. aid receiver understanding.
   c. improve receiver acceptance.
   d. assure sender success.

__________ **7.** The best type(s) of message to use in resolving a minor conflict between two employees would be
   a. written and nonverbal.
   b. nonverbal.
   c. oral and nonverbal.
   d. oral.

_____________ **8.** The receiver
  a. has the responsibility for the success of the communication process.
  b. should be open to different types of senders.
  c. selects the communication channel.
  d. has no responsibility in the communication process.

_____________ **9.** Oral messages should be used
  a. when it is desirable to have a record of the communication.
  b. when the message is complex.
  c. when immediate feedback is desired.
  d. when speed of transmission is not a concern.

_____________ **10.** The major barrier to effective communication is
  a. lack of receiver interest.
  b. failure to use the you–viewpoint.
  c. receiver's lack of knowledge.
  d. poor listening.

Completion

Complete each item by writing the necessary word or words.

1. In the back-and-forth transmission of information you will be both a ____________________
   and a ____________________.

2. The average person spends about ____________________ percent of his or her waking
   hours in some form of communication.

3. The major patterns of business communication are: ____________________,
   ____________________, ____________________,
   ____________________, and ____________________.

4. The sender's role in the communication process includes:
   a. ____________________
   b. ____________________
   c. ____________________
   d. ____________________
   e. ____________________

5. The receiver's role in the communication process includes:
   a. ____________________
   b. ____________________
   c. ____________________
   d. ____________________
   e. ____________________

6. The three basic types of messages are ________________________, ________________________, and ________________________.

7. Using the you–viewpoint means that the sender gives primary consideration to the receiver's point of view when ____.

8. The receiver should be analyzed in four areas: ________________________, ________________________, ________________________, and ________________________.

9. The receiver's interests include ________________________, ________________________, and ________________________.

10. The receiver's values, attitudes, biases, prejudices, and viewpoints are examples of the receiver's ________________________—the third category to be analyzed by the sender.

11. Three important ways for a sender to maintain a favorable relationship with a receiver are:

    a. ____

    b. ____

    c. ____

12. The primary purpose of analyzing the receiver is to enable you to ____.

13. Communication barriers are any factors that ____.

14. List four examples of communication barriers that should be removed so that effective communication can take place.

    ________________________, ________________________, ________________________, and ________________________.

15. The major communication barrier that you as a sender can cause is the ____.

Matching

Write the letter of the best answer in the blank preceding the description. Some answers may be used more than once; others may not be used at all.

_____ **1.** The most important business communication goal	**a.** connotation
_____ **2.** Feedback	**b.** favorable relationship
_____ **3.** Results in the diagonal flow of information	**c.** grapevine
_____ **4.** Message passed along among three or more people	**d.** honesty
_____ **5.** Informal communication	**e.** network
_____ **6.** Is responsible for communication process	**f.** oral message
_____ **7.** Provides greater opportunity for feedback	**g.** planned communication
_____ **8.** Central focus of you–viewpoint	**h.** receiver
_____ **9.** Ethical imperative in communication	**i.** receiver benefits
_____ **10.** Formal communication	**j.** receiver response
	k. receiver understanding
	l. serial communication
	m. sender

Review Questions

1. Explain why business communication is important to individuals.

2. List the four goals of business communication and explain how to achieve each.

3. Indicate the roles of the sender and the receiver in the communication process.

4. Select a person known both to you and to your instructor and analyze that person as a receiver of messages.

5. Create five one-sentence examples of the use of the I–viewpoint. Revise each sentence so that it reflects the you–viewpoint.

APPLICATION EXERCISES

Revise the following sentences so they reflect you–viewpoint writing.

1. We were pleased to receive your application for a VISA® card.

2. You failed to enclose your check with your letter to us.

3. I am sorry we cannot repair your car until Friday.

4. The First National Bank now has a 24-hour teller machine at the Rivercity Mall.

5. It is impossible to sell you a new car before your credit is approved.

6. We proudly manufacture high-quality merchandise.

7. Closing your account with us is a mistake because Jefferson's is going to lower its prices soon.

8. You should move quickly or you will miss the sale of the year.

9. We are glad that you purchase all of your gasoline at BP.

10. You should be aware that Kenwell's does not make refunds on food items that have been un-packed.

11. We want to be sure that our service is the best, and you can help us by stopping by our store and completing our questionnaire.

12. I am pleased to grant your request for a salary increase.

13. It is too bad about the terrible problem you have.

14. Selling toll-free 24 hours per day is our business. You can call us any time at 1 (800) 555-1122.

15. Please write me, and let me know what color to send.

CHAPTER 2

Principles of Business Communication

LEARNING ACTIVITIES

True or False?

Circle T if the statement is true; circle F if the statement is false.

T   F   **1.** The basic principle of business communication is the KISS principle.

T   F   **2.** A thesaurus is a way of finding the simplest and most precise words for a message.

T   F   **3.** For senders and receivers in the same occupation, technical words cannot assist in conveying more effective messages.

T   F   **4.** In some situations negative words can be used for emphasis.

T   F   **5.** Abstract words can be useful if a sender wants to de-emphasize an idea.

T   F   **6.** In letters and memos, a sentence should be considered long if it is 15 words or more.

T   F   **7.** One way to limit content in sentences is to add commas and semicolons to long sentences to make them more readable.

T   F   **8.** Active voice means the sentence is formed in a way to have the subject acted upon.

T   F   **9.** In a report, a paragraph should be considered long if it is 12 lines or more.

T   F   **10.** A sender can effectively emphasize an idea simply by telling the receiver that the idea is important.

Completion

Complete each item by writing the necessary word or words.

1. The best way to improve your ability to compose effective business messages is to learn and use the ____ of business communication.

2. The two most valuable resources or references for the business communicator are a ________________________________ and a ________________________________ .

3. The most effective words you can choose for your messages are those words that your receiver will ______________________________ and that will secure the ______________________________ ______________________________ .

4. Words that are understandable are words that are in your receiver's ______________________________ .

5. Words that have special meanings in a particular field are called ______________________________ .

6. Concrete words are ____ ; abstract words are ______________________________ .

7. The strongest words, or parts of speech, in the English language are ______________________________ and ______________________________ .

8. A sentence that has ______________________________ contains one main idea–one thought.

9. Short sentences should average ______________________________ words in length.

10. Any sentence that exceeds ______________________________ words should be considered a long sentence and should be examined for clarity.

11. In developing sentences, the principle "keep related words together" means that modifiers should be placed ____ .

12. In business letter and memo writing, paragraphs should average ______________________________ lines.

13. If any paragraph in a letter or memo is______________________________ lines or more, it is considered long.

14. In business report writing, paragraphs can average ______________________________ lines.

15. ______________________________ lines or more in any paragraph in a report is long.

Review Questions

1. What are concrete words? Why should you use them in your business communication?

2. What is the difference between strong and weak words? Which are preferred in business communication?

3. Explain the impact of the use of negative words in business messages.

4. Explain how to implement Principle 8: Use Short Sentences. Include in your explanation the recommendation regarding sentence length—short, average, and long—for letters and memos and for reports.

5. What is the difference between the active voice and passive voice in sentences? When should the active voice be used, and when should the passive voice be used?

6. Explain what Principle 11: Use Short Paragraphs means. Include in your discussion the recommendations regarding paragraph length—short, average, and long—for letters and memos and reports.

7. Explain the direct plan and the indirect plan for organizing paragraphs.

8. Explain how you can use transitional words to provide paragraph coherence.

9. What are the three basic types of tie-in sentences that can be used to provide paragraph coherence?

10. You are encouraged to use the 15 principles in Chapter 2 in your business communication. You are also urged to compose with style. How can you do both?

APPLICATION EXERCISES

Assume for these exercises that your receiver is a college freshman with a vocabulary at about the 11th- to 12th-grade level. Your receiver is majoring in business administration.

Be sure to retain the basic meaning of the original words in your revisions. Use examples different from those used in the textbook. Use your dictionary and thesaurus to assist you in these exercises.

1. Select words that will be more *familiar* to your receiver.

    a. habitual ___________________________________

    b. ambiguous ___________________________________

    c. ambivalent ___________________________________

    d. pretentious ___________________________________

    e. nonchalant ___________________________________

2. Choose *shorter* words.

   a. facilitate

   b. lackadaisical

   c. aberration

   d. inaugurate

   e. judicious

3. As appropriate, replace these technical words with *familiar* words.

   a. generate

   b. chronicle

   c. matriculate

   d. jurisdiction

   e. interface

4. Select words that are more *concrete*.

   a. book

   b. country

   c. office equipment

5. Select words that are more *abstract*.

   a. 1,000 miles

   b. A.A. degree

   c. application letter

6. Choose *stronger* words.

   a. ask

   b. prefer

   c. remember

7. Choose *weaker* words.

   a. demand

   b. tactless

   c. repossessed

8. List three positive words and three negative words.

a. ___________________ a. ___________________

b. ___________________ b. ___________________

c. ___________________ c. ___________________

9. Revise these sentences so they are more understandable.

  a. Her proficiency as a writer was incomparable.

  b. Fabricating data is fraudulent.

  c. Optimum arrangements were facilitated for financing Ping-ying's matriculation.

10. Revise these sentences so they are more positive.

  a. Our policy forbids refunds without the sales slip.

  b. We regret that you have decided to quit.

  c. Stop coming in late.

11. Rearrange these sentences so that the modifiers will be in more appropriate locations and the relationships will be clearer.

  a. If the fringe benefits are to be changed, employees before any action is taken will want to be consulted.

  b. Being in dilapidated condition, the ABC Wrecking Company demolished the factory building.

  c. All the employees were reprimanded who were late.

12. Shorten these sentences.

   a. While all the very fine communication equipment is helpful, it remains still very important to compose messages with conciseness and clarity and with clear sentences.

   ____

   ____

   b. The first and initial version of the word processing software was welcomed with open arms.

   ____

   ____

   c. This correspondence is the letter mailed to me, which I received through the mail yesterday.

   ____

   ____

13. Change the voice in these sentences from passive to active.

   a. A truck will be driven to Toledo by Jose Mendez.

   ____

   ____

   b. Finally, the memo was received in the chairperson's office.

   ____

   ____

   c. Jill's concerns were listened to by the appeal officer.

   ____

   ____

14. Create sentences that give the emphasis specified.

   a. Emphasize the low cost of a personal stereo by the length of your sentence.

   ____

   ____

   b. Use format to emphasize the four goals of business communication you learned in Chapter 1.

   ____

   ____

   c. Use sentence structure to emphasize the date of a birthday and to de-emphasize the person's age.

   ____

   ____

15. Improve the unity of the following paragraph by identifying the sentence that does not belong.

When preparing for a job interview, you should learn all you can about the company. In addition, you should try to anticipate all possible questions. Be sure to be on time for the interview. Give attention to the clothes you will wear and your grooming. Possibly the most important preparation you will make is a mental one; a confident attitude is essential for success.

Sentence that does not belong: ____

____

____

____

____

16. Select the most logical order for these sentences so they will form a paragraph that uses the indirect plan.

a. Join PBL today!

b. These new skills and spirit will serve you well all your life.

c. What are the benefits of PBL membership?

d. Through membership you can strengthen your leadership skills and sharpen your competitive edge.

Order: (1) _____ (2) _____ (3) _____ (4) _____

17. Select the most logical order for the sentences in Exercise 16 using the direct plan.

Order: (1) _____ (2) _____ (3) _____ (4) _____

18. Provide coherence for the following paragraph by inserting the appropriate transitional words or tie-in sentences.

The personnel officer called and said she wanted to talk to Pete. She said he is being considered for a job. She said that the call was about an interview. She asked that Pete return the call. Her instructions were that he should do so as soon as possible.

With coherence: ____

____

____

____

____

____

____

19. Restore coherence to the following paragraph by reordering the sentences so that they provide for a flow of thought and the logical movement of the reader's mind from one idea to the next. Indicate your order by placing the letters of the sentences in the blanks provided.

(a) To increase market share and gain the profit that goes with it, a business must have managers who are ethical, alert, tough, dynamic, creative, persevering, and energetic. (b) In fact, the market share must increase if a business is to grow and prosper. (c) Ways must continually be found to regain any lost market share and the profit that goes with it. (d) That environment includes the appearance of new competitors with new and better ideas for attracting customers. (e) These kinds of managers make profits and make businesses successful. (f) A business must make a profit to be successful. (g) This essential profit is fought for in a challenging, competitive environment. (h) These new competitors take a share of the market.

Order: (1) _____ (2) _____ (3) _____ (4) _____ (5) _____ (6) _____ (7) _____ (8) _____

20. Improve the dull, stiff, lifeless, I–viewpoint style of this paragraph. Write your improved version using the direct plan.

I received your complaint letter. We have thought through what happened and found that the shipment was lost. I talked to the freight company about it; I believe I can get our money back. Therefore, the good news for you, I guess, is that you can have the refund you asked for. With best regards,

<hr>

CHAPTER 3

Developing Business Messages

LEARNING ACTIVITIES

True or False?

Circle T if the statement is true; circle F if the statement is false.

T   F   **1.** Step 1 in Planning and Composing Business Messages includes analyzing the receiver for the you–viewpoint.

T   F   **2.** When using the you–viewpoint, give highest priority to what you think will be your receiver's perception of the message.

T   F   **3.** An advantage of oral messages is that they are more personal.

T   F   **4.** You should use the direct plan for persuasive messages.

T   F   **5.** When drafting a message, it is important to get it just right in order to avoid editing, revising, and proofreading later.

T   F   **6.** The middle-level receiver's vocabulary will fall between grade levels 8 and 10.

T   F   **7.** Being ethical in your business communication includes striving for the highest good attainable for all those involved in the communication.

T   F   **8.** Because business communicators cannot be expected to know all the laws that affect their communication, they should ask that routine messages be reviewed by an attorney.

T   F   **9.** "Men are 27 percent stronger than women," is an example of biased language.

T   F   **10.** The English language has a gender-biased structure.

Multiple Choice

Write the letter that represents the best answer in the blank at the left.

__________ 1. The primary and secondary purposes of a message are the
   a. direct and indirect plans.
   b. main idea and supporting ideas.
   c. you–viewpoint and vocabulary level.
   d. first and second content items.

__________ 2. An advantage of a written message is that it
   a. is quickly transmitted.
   b. is more personal.
   c. allows immediate feedback.
   d. accommodates lengthy and complex content.

__________ 3. The indirect approach should be used for most messages that contain
   a. positive and neutral information.
   b. neutral and persuasive information.
   c. negative and persuasive information.
   d. positive and persuasive information.

__________ 4. Which of the following statements is biased?
   a. The average height of women is less than the average height of men.
   b. The African-American student spoke about his race.
   c. The old woman was in the hospital.
   d. The Hispanic-American student especially enjoyed the talk on Mexican history.

__________ 5. When used in ethical decision making, the social utility concept requires a communicator to
   a. determine the greatest good and the least harm for all affected.
   b. follow the guidance of the standards of society at large.
   c. follow the universal law that applies.
   d. assess the situation using the Golden Rule.

__________ 6. Readability formulas
   a. indicate the vocabulary level at which a message is written.
   b. measure the average length of sentences, the percentage of difficult words in a message, and the accuracy of the message.
   c. check the actual words used in a message.
   d. determine the manner in which words are combined into sentences in messages.

__________ 7. Express warranties of products and services are established by
   a. salesperson statements to the customer.
   b. statements of the customer during a transaction.
   c. customer requests in writing.
   d. businesses putting guarantees in writing.

_______ **8.** Employment communication is most influenced by which of the following pieces of legislation?
  a. Civil Rights Act
  b. Plain English laws
  c. Labor-Management Relations Act
  d. The Privacy Act

_______ **9.** Use of the generic word *man*
  a. should be avoided in business messages.
  b. represents men and women as equals.
  c. is necessary to avoid stereotyping.
  d. cannot be eliminated because there are no acceptable alternatives.

_______ **10.** Which is the best wording in the following examples?
  a. The ladies and the men
  b. The man and wife
  c. The ladies and the gentlemen
  d. The men and the girls

Completion

Complete each item by writing in the necessary word or words.

1. The process for planning and composing all types of written and oral business messages is the same. The three steps in the process are:

   a. to determine ____.

   b. to analyze the receiver for the ____________________________.

   c. to compose ____.

2. When a team of writers develops a message the process is called ________________________ ____.

3. The first step in developing messages has two tasks:

   a. Analyze the _______________________________________.

   b. Establish ____________________________ and ____________________________ purposes.

4. The receiver should be analyzed in four areas:

   ____________________________ , ____________________________ , ____________________________ , and ____________________________.

5. Using the you–viewpoint means choosing words that are ____________________________ and ____________________________ to your receiver.

6. To achieve the purpose(s) of a message that will be sent to multiple receivers, the message should be composed at the ______________________________ level that can be understood by all members of the group.

7. The receiver's ______________________________ of your message is your message.

8. The three main advantages of oral messages are that they ______________________________ ______________________________, ______________________________ ______________________________, and ______________________________ ______________________________.

9. The two organizational plans for messages are the ______________________________ plan and the ______________________________ plan.

10. The two parts involved in the task of outlining message content are ______________________________ ______________________________ and ______________________________ ______________________________.

11. After the content of the message has been outlined, the next task is to ______________________________ the message.

12. When editing and revising, keep the ______________________________ and ______________________________ purposes of the message in mind.

13. Careful proofreading involves:

    a. reading the message for ______________________________.

    b. reading it again for correct ______________________________, ______________________________, and ______________________________.

14. A readability formula indicates the ______________________________ ______________________________ at which a message is written.

15. Business messages written at the ______________________________ to the ______________________________ grade levels will communicate clearly with most receivers.

16. Most high school graduates' vocabulary levels will be at grade levels ______________________________ to ______________________________.

17. Being ethical is doing what is ______________________________ to achieve what is ______________________________.

18. The ______________________________ concept requires that communicators be willing to require all others to behave as they are behaving.

19. If you are not sure about the legality of one of your messages, you should consult an ______________________________ or other ______________________________.

   Chapter 3 • Developing Business Messages

20. Biased language offends ____ and

____________________________________.

APPLICATION EXERCISES

Improve the following sentences by editing and revising them.

1. The soldiers they are tired and weary.

2. Once the plan is completed and the plan is finalized the plan will be submitted to management.

3. Communication has a power that, for all intents and purposes, is not equaled by anything else.

4. Do you think that it is time for a meeting so we can get together and discuss relevant and appropriate plans for new products?

5. At some point in the future, Paul will be put in line to be named president of the company.

Proofread the following sentences. Rewrite each sentence correcting the errors you found.

6. Tri too finde thee problims in this sentince.

7. Schedulse help or ganizes the work

8. She think thet the produuction qota wil bea meet

9. the questions askt bi the student's wer good wones

10. is the end of maple street were marked withe a detoor sign

Eliminate the biased language in the following sentences:

11. Most Americans are overly compulsive about being on time.

12. When a person is prepared, he can succeed.

13. The cancer patients are encouraged to call 1-800 ANSWERS if they have questions.

14. If a salesman wants to do well, he will know his product thoroughly.

15. The black student suggested that the test be on Friday.

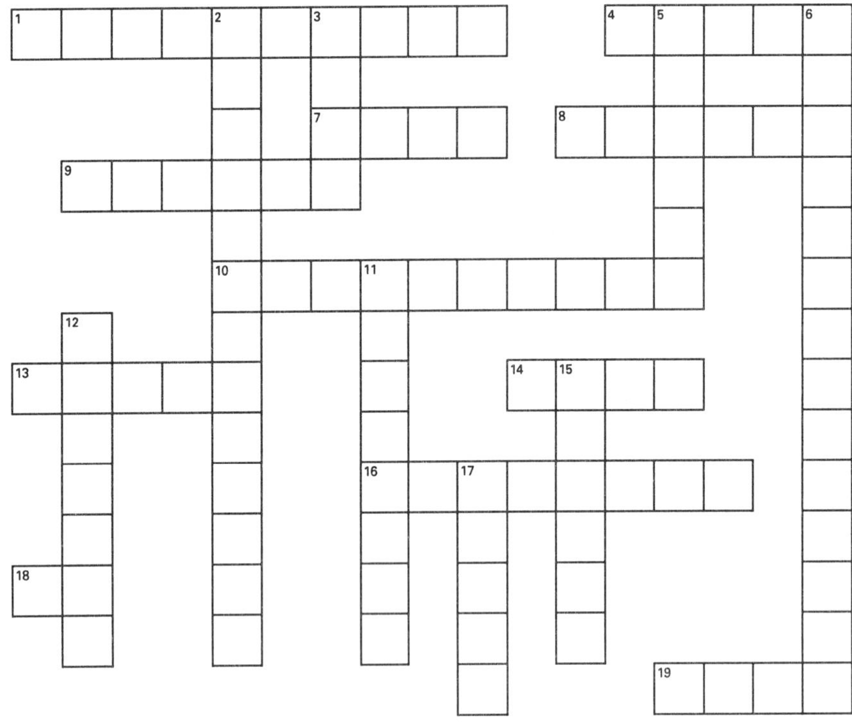

Across

1. The words that one knows
4. Lying that causes monetary damage
7. _______ processing equipment
8. Readability _______
9. Moral code or values
10. To put people in categories
13. Ethical philosophy
14. A way to strengthen a message
16. An organizational plan for a message
18. Male pronoun
19. The message's _______ idea is its primary purpose.

Down

2. Technique for creating ideas
3. Legal requirements
5. Edit and _______ messages
6. Prohibited by the Civil Rights Act
11. Listener or reader
12. Type of message
15. An organizational plan for a message
17. First effort at composing a message

CHAPTER 4

Communication
Technologies
and
Techniques

LEARNING ACTIVITIES

True or False?

Circle T if the statement is true; circle F if the statement is false.

T   F   **1.** Reduced communication costs and increased worker productivity are benefits of technology.

T   F   **2.** The document cycle begins with creation and ends with filing, storage, and retrieval.

T   F   **3.** E-mail may be used to send a message locally or internationally.

T   F   **4.** Fax transmissions can be made using paper or a computer.

T   F   **5.** While visiting the scene of a house fire and preparing a report about it, an insurance agent would most likely use a touchscreen as a computer input device.

T   F   **6.** Document analysis software detects and corrects grammar and punctuation errors.

T   F   **7.** Windows software is most efficient when accessed through a programmable keyboard.

T   F   **8.** Group Decision Support Systems help business professionals make effective oral presentations.

T   F   **9.** Plain form messages should be keyed, printed, proofread, and signed before being duplicated.

T   F   **10.** Guide messages should be used for routine correspondence that needs to be modified to fit specialized circumstances.

Completion

1. The _______________________ and the _______________________ are computer
   pointing devices.

2. A bar-code reader is a hand-held _______________________.

3. Because they fit easily into briefcases, _______________________ computers are popular
   among business travelers.

4. The thesaurus and spell checker are two popular features of
   _______________________ software.

5. The two printer types are _______________________ and _______________________.

6. _______________________ is much smaller than paper output, but special equipment is
   needed to read it.

7. _______________________ connect computers within a small area; _______________________
   connect computers in distant locations.

8. Form messages, guide messages, and form paragraphs are identified by
   _______________________ assigned at the time the items are created.

9. Avoid using only the _______________________ and the _______________________ as
   variables in fill-in form messages.

10. The most expensive mail service is _______________________ mail.

Matching

Write the letter of the best answer in the blank preceding the term. Some answers may be used more than once; others may not be used at all.

_________ **1.** monitor type

_________ **2.** spreadsheet data location

_________ **3.** information that changes

_________ **4.** links a computer, 35mm camera, and a film recorder

_________ **5.** message containing several options that apply to one situation

_________ **6.** alternative to individually keyed mailing envelopes

_________ **7.** message with full content prepared in advance but not printed until needed

_________ **8.** allows greatest content flexibility in a message

_________ **9.** uses a speech synthesizer

_________ **10.** most advanced form of conferencing

a. audio conferencing

b. cell

c. checklist form message

d. desktop slidemaker

e. form paragraphs

f. guide message

g. labels

h. LCD

i. pagers

j. variable

k. video output

l. video conferencing

m. voice output

APPLICATION EXERCISES

1. Assume that you own a real estate agency. You currently have 77 listings and your client base is expanding. You have noticed that your correspondence has become more routine; occasionally, you prepare a message that is repetitive. Answer the following questions for each situation:

    (1) Is the message routine, repetitive, or both? Why?

    (2) Should you create a form message (be specific about type), guide message, or form paragraphs? Why?

    (3) Should the finished message(s) be distributed by first- class or by third-class mail? Why?

    a. Whenever someone lists a home for sale through your agency, you want to send a letter thanking them for their business.

    b. Whenever you sell a house, you want to inform people in the immediate area of the sale and let them know who their new neighbors are.

    c. You wish to announce your candidacy for President of the local Association of Realtors and ask members to vote for you.

    d. You wish to invite the buyers with whom you are currently working to attend a Saturday morning workshop on home mortgage financing.

2. In each of the following sentences, underline the word or words that could become variables if the sentence were included as part of a guide message or a series of guide paragraphs.

    a. The credit limit on your account is $5,000 and the interest rate is 13 percent.

    b. Please complete the questionnaire and return it by May 31.

    c. The next meeting of the committee will be held on Monday, June 17, in Room 212.

    d. Before he may enter kindergarten, Rodrigo must be immunized for measles.

    e. This amount includes tuition for 15 credits at $66 each and the universal student service fee of $120.

3. After reading the following paragraphs, underline the errors that would not have been detected by a spell checker.

    Tank your four at tending the in vestment seminar held on September 33. Mr. Amy Bockworth is an excellent presenter; you are confident you grained much from her presentation.

    Ms. Bockworth indicated hat you were interested in baying a copy if *Money Madness*, the book she rote. An order form is enclosed. Simple return the farm with you check fore $12.9, and well process your order immediately.

4. Which of the following form paragraphs should be used in preparing messages to meet situations *a* through *d*? Focus your attention on overall content, not paragraph sequencing.

Number   Paragraph (variables underlined)

1   Your copy of the sales report for the _number_ quarter is attached. Please review the report and share its contents with your staff.

2   Congratulations! Your area was the sales leader for the _number_ quarter.

3   The figures for this quarter reflect an increase in sales of $ _amount_ for your area.

4   Please review the attached sales report for the _number_ quarter and share it with your staff.

5   The figures indicate that your area had an increase in sales of $ _amount_. This increase represents a fine recovery.

6   The sales summary for the _number_ quarter has been completed, _name of sales manager_, and we are concerned about what the figures indicate.

7   Your area has once again suffered a loss in sales. The figures show that your area experienced a decrease in sales of $ _amount_.

8   The sales figures for the _number_ quarter show that your area experienced a decrease in sales of $ _amount_.

9   The sales figures for the _number_ quarter show that your area experienced an increase in sales of $ _amount_. This is the _number_ consecutive quarter in which you have shown an increase.

10   Thank you! Keep up the good work.

11   Your area has a great sales potential, and you have done well with it.

12   Your area has a great sales potential, and we want you to do well with it. If there is anything this office can do to help you, please let us know.

13   Plan to attend the sales managers' meeting on _date_ in _location_. Sales strategies will be the primary agenda item.

a.   District 12, managed by Tiffany Lorenz, was the sales leader during the second quarter. Sales totaled $155,882 during the three-month period. You'll attach a copy of the report with your memo.

b.   Marvin Wegg joined the firm as manager of District 3. He joined the firm five months ago and sales in his district have risen by $21,067 over the last quarter. You're glad to see the improvement in this district, which has had unrealized sales potential.

c.   T. T. Sloane has been with the company longer than Marvin Wegg but hasn't experienced much success. This quarter his district saw a $993 decrease in sales. A decrease in sales of less than $1000 may not seem like much, but District 8 has experienced declines in sales for three quarters in a row. T. T. is one of the managers you want to see at the sales strategy meeting to be held early next month.

d. District 11, managed by Mark Radjui, is a consistent producer. During the past three months, this area increased its sales by \$93,210. This increase, although impressive, is not enough to make District 11 the sales leader. Still, Mr. Radjui and his staff should be pleased with their success.

CHAPTER 5

International and Cross-Cultural Business Communication

LEARNING ACTIVITIES

True or False?

Circle T if the statement is true; circle F if the statement is false.

T   F   **1.** Most students today will be involved in international and cross-cultural business communication at some time during their careers.

T   F   **2.** *Americans* is a term used throughout the world to refer to citizens of the United States.

T   F   **3.** More than 20,000 languages are spoken throughout the world.

T   F   **4.** American manufacturers have made serious, costly errors because of their lack of knowledge of other cultures.

T   F   **5.** There is less variation in nonverbal signals than there is in language.

T   F   **6.** Some acceptable and common nonverbal signals in one culture may be vulgar in another culture.

T   F   **7.** The way that people feel and think is the most important cultural difference in cross-cultural communication.

T   F   **8.** The goal of cross-cultural communication is to achieve normal business communication without cultural prejudice.

T   F   **9.** The key guideline for cross-cultural communication is to analyze your own culture.

T   F   **10.** Stereotypes of other cultures are largely inaccurate and not useful.

T	F	**11.** The study of cultural relativism indicates that there is not necessarily one right or wrong way to do something—merely many different, but equally correct, ways.
T	F	**12.** If you know only a few words of another person's language, it is better not to use them until you know enough of the language to construct sentences.
T	F	**13.** When using an interpreter, be careful of the words you use and do not let the interpreter convey just the meaning of your message.
T	F	**14.** When in Rome do as the Romans do, is an appropriate adage for international businesspersons to follow.
T	F	**15.** High-quality translation software is available to translate from one language to another.

Multiple Choice

Write the letter that represents the best answer in the blank at the left.

__________ **1.** The number of cultures estimated to exist in the world is
  a. 2,000.
  b. 5,000.
  c. 10,000.
  d. 20,000.

__________ **2.** In Japan the most acceptable nonverbal greeting is
  a. shaking hands.
  b. an embrace.
  c. a bow.
  d. the wai.

__________ **3.** Among the following cultural attributes, the one(s) the Japanese value most highly is/are
  a. individual achievement.
  b. human relationships.
  c. directness.
  d. business relationships.

__________ **4.** Most international business communication is conducted in
  a. Spanish.
  b. English.
  c. French.
  d. German.

_________ **5.** The culture that is least likely to base moral judgments on absolute ethical standards
is
   a. American.
   b. Canadian.
   c. German.
   d. Japanese.

_________ **6.** The culture that is most likely to have members who are basically conservative and
who prefer discipline and order to change is
   a. American.
   b. Canadian.
   c. German.
   d. Japanese.

_________ **7.** The United States' largest trading partner is
   a. Canada.
   b. Mexico.
   c. Japan.
   d. Germany.

_________ **8.** Mexicans are likely to achieve self-esteem primarily through
   a. approval of superiors.
   b. friendships and personal relationships.
   c. achievement on the job.
   d. individual accomplishment.

_________ **9.** The fastest growing American subculture is
   a. African-American.
   b. Hispanic.
   c. American Indian.
   d. Asian-American.

_________ **10.** The source of information that most likely has the most extensive publications on
cross-cultural communication is
   a. Association for Business Communication.
   b. International Association of Business Communicators.
   c. David M. Kennedy Center for International Studies.
   d. International Business Publishing Company.

Matching

Write the letter of the best answer in the blank preceding the term. Each answer may be used only one time.

__________ 1. Bow	**a.** bird
__________ 2. "Marks" in Canada	**b.** stoic
__________ 3. Wai	**c.** bending gently with palms together below chin
__________ 4. Namaste	**d.** bending at the waist
__________ 5. Australian emu	**e.** greeting in Thailand
__________ 6. Hispanics	**f.** through friends in Mexico
__________ 7. Eye contact	**g.** more important in Japan than business relations
__________ 8. American Indians	**h.** necessary in France
__________ 9. Personal trust	**i.** likely to use first language
__________ 10. Self-esteem	**j.** school grades
	k. upward movement of the head

Completion

Complete each item by writing the necessary word or words.

1. Cross-cultural communication means communication between members of ________________ ____.

2. *Cultural relativism* means that different cultures have different ________________________ ____.

3. The variation among receivers' cultures in the world includes differences in ____, ____, and ____. (List only three.)

4. Members of the Japanese culture practice ____ ____ ethics.

5. When communicating with Germans, Americans should generally be ___________________________,
   ___________________________________, ___________________________________, and
   _______________________________.

6. In international business communication, there is as much variation among the meanings of
   _______________________________ signals as there is variation among languages.

7. The most important difference among cultures to consider in cross-cultural communication is
   the way people ____.

8. In cross-cultural communication situations, the basic business communication knowledge you
   have already gained (will, will not) _______________________________ apply.

9. A starting point in preparing yourself to communicate with persons from another culture is
   Guideline 2: ____.

10. There is considerable evidence that Americans think in an _______________________________
    manner.

Review Questions

1. Why are American businesses becoming more involved in world trade?

2. Describe the language differences throughout the world.

3. Describe the differences in nonverbal signals throughout the world.

4. Give an example that illustrates a difference between the American mainstream culture and each
   of the following American subcultures: (a) African-American, (b) Hispanic, and (c) American
   Indian.

5. Describe the differences in business hours and days in countries throughout the world.

6. To be successful in international and cross-cultural business communication, you are encouraged to learn all you can about other cultures and then apply what you learn. What are examples
   of the kinds of things you should learn about other cultures?

7. Give five examples of behavior appropriate for a business meeting with Japanese businesspersons.

8. Give five examples of behavior appropriate for a business meeting with German businesspersons.

9. How are citizens of Mexico different from citizens of the United States? Give five examples.

10. How are citizens of Canada different from citizens of the United States? Give five examples.

CHAPTER 7

Sentence Structure

LEARNING ACTIVITIES

True or False?

Circle T if the statement is true; circle F if the statement is false.

T   F   **1.** A sentence is a group of related words that expresses a complete thought.

T   F   **2.** The subject of the sentence is the part that expresses action or state of being.

T   F   **3.** The complete predicate includes the main verb in the sentence and all the words directly related to it.

T   F   **4.** When analyzing sentences, you should locate the subject first.

T   F   **5.** In inverted sentences the verb precedes the subject.

T   F   **6.** The direct object receives the action of the verb and answers the *what?* or *whom?* question raised by the subject and the verb.

T   F   **7.** A subject complement can be a predicate that modifies the subject.

T   F   **8.** The phrase *bright and quick* is an adjective phrase.

T   F   **9.** A dependent clause contains a subject or a predicate.

T   F   **10.** An independent clause can stand alone as a separate sentence.

T   F   **11.** If you add a subordinate conjunction to a dependent clause, it will become an independent clause.

T   F   **12.** If a subject in a sentence is singular, the predicate in that sentence may be either singular or plural.

T   F   **13.** Pronouns and their antecedents must agree in number.

T   F   **14.** Parallelism in a sentence means having agreement between the subject and the predicate and between a pronoun and its antecedent.

T   F   **15.** The five purposes of sentences include questions, statements, suggestions, commands, and exclamations.

Multiple Choice

Write the letter that represents the best answer in the blank at the left.

__________   **1.** Which of the following choices represents the main parts of sentences?
- **a.** Subject and predicate
- **b.** Verb and predicate
- **c.** Subject and object
- **d.** Phrases and clauses

__________   **2.** Which of the following sentences has the complete predicate capitalized?
- **a.** MARTHA, the personnel manager, carefully read the report.
- **b.** Martha, the personnel manager, CAREFULLY READ THE REPORT.
- **c.** Martha, the personnel manager, carefully read THE REPORT.
- **d.** MARTHA, THE PERSONNEL MANAGER, carefully read the report.

__________   **3.** Which of the following sentences has the simple subject capitalized?
- **a.** MARTHA, the personnel manager, carefully read the report.
- **b.** Martha, the personnel manager, CAREFULLY READ THE REPORT.
- **c.** Martha, the personnel manager, carefully read THE REPORT.
- **d.** MARTHA, THE PERSONNEL MANAGER, carefully read the report.

__________   **4.** Subject complements
- **a.** receive the action of the subject.
- **b.** rename or modify the subject.
- **c.** receive the action of the verb.
- **d.** rename or modify the verb.

__________   **5.** A dependent clause
- **a.** includes a subject and a verb.
- **b.** can stand alone.
- **c.** does not include both a subject and a verb.
- **d.** can function as a part of speech.

__________   **6.** In which of the following sentences does the subject not agree with the verb?
- **a.** The manager calls a meeting.
- **b.** They were assembled quickly.
- **c.** The employees, particularly Lila, was pleased.
- **d.** The supervisors, including Scott and Josh, report each morning.

_____________ 7. In which of the following sentences does the pronoun not agree with its antecedent?
   a. Either Edna or Pam will take her car on the trip.
   b. The proposal raises some questions; it will have to be revised.
   c. The University will revise their rules on class attendance.
   d. The men and women took their vacations in December.

_____________ 8. Which of the following sentences has parallel construction?
   a. Lori is an accurate and fast keyboard operator.
   b. Lori is an accurate keyboard operator and is fast.
   c. Lori is fast and an accurate keyboard operator.
   d. Lori is a fast and an accurate keyboard operator.

_____________ 9. What is the purpose of the following sentence: Make sure that the time clock is set properly before the employees come to work tomorrow.
   a. Declarative
   b. Interrogative
   c. Imperative
   d. Exclamatory

_____________ 10. What type of sentence is the following: When any CompacCo customer raises a question about our company's ethics, we can point to our creed and provide several anecdotes reflecting ethical employee behavior.
   a. Simple sentence
   b. Compound sentence
   c. Complex sentence
   d. Compound-complex sentence

Completion

Complete each sentence by writing the necessary word or words in the blanks.

1. The two main parts of sentences are the _____________________________ and the _____________________________.

2. The subject is that part of a sentence that tells _____________________________.

3. The predicate is that part of a sentence that includes the verb and tells _____________________________.

4. The name of the clause that expresses a complete thought and has a subject and a predicate is _____________________________.

5. The name of the clause that cannot stand alone as a complete thought is _____________________________.

6. Write an example of a sentence fragment that might be used in a business message. _____________________________.

7. The subject and predicate in a sentence must agree in ___________________________________.

8. If the antecedent is the word *conference*, then the pronoun must be ___________________________.

9. Parallelism means having balance and consistency between or among parts of sentences that ___________________________________.

10. The complex sentence structure permits the writer to ___________________________________ ideas in the same sentence.

APPLICATION EXERCISES

Parts of Sentences. Follow the directions for identifying the parts of sentences specified in each of the following sets of exercises.

Underline the complete subject.

1. Both Antwan and Maurice are over six feet tall.

2. The new employee carefully presented the report.

3. The 40 computers in the laboratory worked perfectly.

Underline the simple subject.

4. Both Antwan and Maurice are over six feet tall.

5. The new employee carefully presented the report.

6. The 40 computers in the laboratory worked perfectly.

Underline the complete predicate.

7. Both Antwan and Maurice are over six feet tall.

8. The new employee carefully presented the report.

9. The 40 computers in the laboratory worked perfectly.

Underline the simple predicate.

10. Both Antwan and Maurice are over six feet tall.

11. The new employee carefully presented the report.

12. The 40 computers in the laboratory worked perfectly.

Underline the direct object if one is present.

13. Fortunately, some will realize profit.

14. The employee wrote the memo to Harry.

15. Every report is accurate.

Underline the indirect object if one is present.

16. Take the evidence to the customer.

17. Bring all the employees meals for the picnic.

18. The instructor assigned the students term papers to write.

Underline the subject complement if one is present.

19. Lynn is an outstanding manager.

20. As a manager, he brought a new spirit to the factory.

21. Tracy is strong.

Identify each of the following phrases.

22. to see   __________________________________

23. of the group   __________________________________

24. old and decrepit   __________________________________

25. should have bought   __________________________________

26. a comprehensive report   __________________________________

27. speaking rapidly   __________________________________

Indicate whether each of the following items is an independent clause, a dependent clause, or a phrase.

28. if you attended the ball game   __________________________________

29. the company picnic was well attended   __________________________________

30. on the table   __________________________________

Subject and Verb Agreement. Underline the correct verb in each of the following sentences.

1. The members (attend, attends) the reception.

2. The clerk with the papers (is, are) the main bookkeeper.

3. Neither the members nor the clerk (know, knows) who attended.

4. "Battles" (was, were) an off-Broadway production.

5. Many (select, selects) the first offer.

6. The task force (agree, agrees) with the administration.

7. The students and the vice president (feel, feels) differently.

8. Both (was, were) willing to debate further.

9. He said, "$2 million (is, are) the cost."

10. The students or the vice president (plan, plans) to meet with the president.

Pronoun and Antecedent Agreement. Underline the correct pronoun in each of the following sentences.

1. Sam's Wholesale Discount Store will open (its, their) new Mayfield store on March 10.

2. Alice and Frank are taking (her and his, their) vacations soon.

3. One should complete (his or her, its) work before vacationing.

4. Either Richard or Frank will bring (his, their) report.

5. Richard and Frank will bring (his, their) report.

Functions of Sentences. Write in the blanks at the right the purpose (statement, command, question, or exclamation) of each of the following sentences. Also provide the correct ending punctuation for each sentence.

1. Hurry ________________________________

2. The firm was successful ________________________________

3. Move the fax machine to the desk ________________________________

4. When can you call ________________________________

5. Please take a message for me ________________________________

Types of Sentence Structures. Indicate the structure (simple, compound, complex, or compound-complex) for each of the following sentences.

1. When the siren sounds, the factory work stops and employees leave the building; the emergency system works well. _______________________________

2. The tasks were listed, and the staff was ready to work. _______________________________

3. Although tired, the men and women assigned to the factory continued to work until the stereo order was completed and shipped to the customer. _______________________________

4. Both Joe's and Darrell's names are in the final list of candidates that is posted on the bulletin board. _______________________________

5. The city is where the action is. _______________________________

WORD PUZZLE

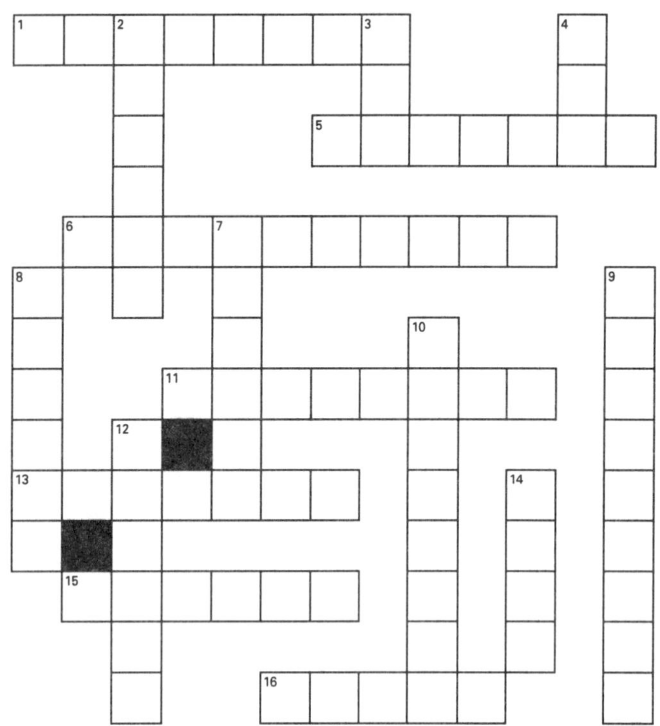

Across

1. Incomplete sentence
5. Has dependent clause and independent clause
6. Renames the subject
11. _____, Krizan, and Merrier—your textbook authors
13. Main noun or pronoun
15. A pronoun and its antecedent must agree in _________
16. State of _____

Down

2. A verb expresses _____
3. A compound sentence has _____ clause(s)
4. A complex sentence has _____ independent clause(s)
7. Has either subject or verb
8. Has both subject and verb
9. Introduced by subordinate conjunction
10. Interrogative sentence
12. There are two types: direct and indirect
14. Expresses action

CHAPTER 8

Punctuation

LEARNING ACTIVITIES

True or False?

Circle T if the statement is true; circle F if the statement is false.

T F **1.** A courteous request may end with either a period or a question mark.

T F **2.** An indirect question is a request that calls for action rather than an oral or written response.

T F **3.** Using commas incorrectly can hamper communication.

T F **4.** A comma is used in a complex sentence only when the dependent clause introduces the independent clause.

T F **5.** To test whether a series of adjectives independently modify the same noun, a writer should insert *and* between them.

T F **6.** A complete geographic location consists of a city, state, and ZIP Code.

T F **7.** Placement in a sentence determines whether words and phrases, such as *however, therefore*, and *of course*, are parenthetical or transitional expressions.

T F **8.** Some writers prefer to use *that* to begin a restrictive clause and *which* to begin a nonrestrictive clause.

T F **9.** Commas and semicolons may be used interchangeably to separate items in a series.

T F **10.** Appositives, whether essential or nonessential, are separated from the rest of a sentence by commas.

Multiple Choice

Write the letter that represents the best answer in the blank at the left.

_____________ **1.** Two closely related independent clauses should be linked by a
       a. comma.
       b. dash.
       c. period.
       d. semicolon.

_____________ **2.** Which of the following punctuation marks is used to *separate*?
       a. Dash
       b. Diagonal
       c. Hyphen
       d. Ellipsis points

_____________ **3.** The hyphen is used
       a. to form coordinate adjectives.
       b. to join numbers or letters in a range.
       c. to separate prefixes and suffixes from root words.
       d. to show a sudden change in thought.

_____________ **4.** Which of the following punctuation marks is *least* emphatic?
       a. Comma
       b. Dash
       c. Parentheses
       d. Underscore

_____________ **5.** Which of the following items should be displayed in quotation marks?
       a. A paraphrased statement
       b. A technical term used in a nontechnical way
       c. The title of a book
       d. The title of a painting

_____________ **6.** What determines whether a direct quotation is displayed in commas or as an indented paragraph?
       a. Its length
       b. The writer's preference
       c. The source from which the quote is taken
       d. The space available on the page

_____________ **7.** Which punctuation mark is always placed *inside* quotation marks?
       a. Colon
       b. Exclamation point
       c. Period
       d. Semicolon

_________ **8.** Which punctuation mark is used as a substitute for italics?
  a. Colon
  b. Parentheses
  c. Quotation marks
  d. Underscore

_________ **9.** Which punctuation mark is so emphatic it should be used sparingly in business writing?
  a. Colon
  b. Dash
  c. Hyphen
  d. Underscore

_________ **10.** When used in advertising, ellipsis points
  a. give emphasis to what follows.
  b. introduce a paraphrased statement.
  c. indicate a pause.
  d. end an indirect quotation.

APPLICATION EXERCISES

Terminal Punctuation

As you read the memo below, you will notice that there are no terminal punctuation marks. A blank line has been inserted to show where sentences and questions end. Insert the appropriate terminal punctuation mark on each line.

TO: Unit Supervisors

FROM: Nicholas J. Memb, Contract Administrator *N. M.*

DATE: July 15, 199-

SUBJECT: CLARIFICATION OF VACATION AND SICK LEAVE POLICIES

During the past several weeks, many of you have come to me with questions about how to interpret the vacation and sick leave sections of the recently ratified bargaining unit contract ______ The information below should help clarify the way in which the policies are to be applied ______

How are vacation and sick leave accrued ______

Employees who have been with the company for less than 5 years earn 4 hours of vacation and 4 hours of sick leave each pay period—12 days of each per year ______ Those who have been with the company 5 or more years earn 4 hours of sick leave and 6 hours of vacation each pay period—12 days of sick leave and 18 days of vacation each year ______

When do new employees become eligible for these benefits ______

New employees begin to accrue both sick leave and vacation time during the first payroll period they are employed ______ They may use their sick leave as it is accumulated but must wait until they have been employed six months before using accrued vacation ______

Must leave be taken only in full-day increments ______

Both sick leave and vacation may be used in increments as small as one hour ______ An employee who has an appointment with a doctor, for example, might use only two hours of sick leave ______

May sick leave be used to care for an ill child ______

Sick leave may be used to care for any dependent (child, parent, spouse, or life partner) who is ill ______

May employees use sick leave for vacations ______

At this time sick leave may be used only for illness or other medical reason ______ The possibility of allowing employees who have accrued unusually large amounts of sick leave to convert a portion of their accumulated leave to vacation will be discussed in two years when we negotiate the next contract ______

Please phone me if you have additional questions about the contract language ______

lb

Internal Punctuation

Some of the following sentences require internal punctuation. Insert commas and semicolons where needed.

1. Indeed many good cellular phone systems are available.

2. Because of the Memorial Day holiday there will be no mail delivery on Monday however mail deposited at the Atlantic Street postal station before 5 p.m. will be processed.

3. Only a few consultants specialize in solar-power automotive technology now but the number is growing at a steady rate.

4. Simply complete and mail the enclosed card today it requires no postage.

5. For further information phone or write our representative in Mountain View California Salem Oregon or Tempe Arizona.

6. Please add my name to your list of members and let me know when the first meeting will be held.

7. You could live without food for weeks but you could survive only a few days without water.

8. A market gap exists our product is designed to fill it.

9. The ordinance about which you inquired was repealed in July 1989.

10. Quality improvement workshops will be held in Room 107 at 2 p.m. Tuesday 9 a.m. Wednesday and 7 p.m. Thursday.

11. Rubin Shirley and Herman will ride with Hanna Abe Ina and Elsie will ride with Cecil.

12. The main office is in Houston Texas the manufacturing plants are located in Boise Idaho Muncie Indiana and Dunedin Florida.

13. To keep the meeting as brief as possible each committee should prepare and distribute a copy of its report ten days in advance.

14. Reading about the procedure provides some insight to completely understand it however you must perform it.

15. Your generous contribution will enable us to purchase bright shiny red bicycles for four needy children in our community.

16. No consensus about how to modify the document could be reached therefore the current policy will continue.

17. If you conduct a thorough investigation the mystery will certainly be solved.

18. One of the apartments is vacant and we can view it anytime the other is occupied but the tenant will allow us to view it if we are there at 10 a.m. on Tuesday morning.

19. Thank you Brenna for responding so quickly to our request.

20. When you are ready to add Susan to your account phone Marlys Alvarado.

Internal Punctuation

Each of the following sentences requires internal punctuation. Insert commas, semicolons, apostrophes, colons, dashes, diagonals, ellipsis points, hyphens, parentheses, periods, quotation marks, and underscores where needed.

1. People who practice time management techniques believe progress can be made in 10 or 15 minute time blocks therefore they don't waste time at the end of the day before lunch or before coffee breaks.

2. Figures are presented for eight cities Chicago Illinois Green Bay Madison and Milwaukee Wisconsin Richmond Virginia San Francisco and Los Angeles California and Lexington Kentucky.

3. The cost of EVLs efficient effective virus detection software program has been reduced.

4. The training material should be designed so that it meets the companys specific needs.

5. Installation will be easy if you follow the step by step instructions on the enclosed form.

6. The Model 826 is our best selling vacuum the Model 729 is our least expensive.

7. The American Business Association ABA will hold one of its regional conferences in Des Moines Iowa.

8. When ordered in quantities of 100 or more "Tax Tips for Professionals is available for only 5 cents copy.

9. Paul said that nifty keen and slick were popular slang terms when he was young.

10. The renewal notice I received indicated that $1299 was . . . the lowest rate available anywhere" for a one year subscription to the magazine.

11. Your request for a three month leave of absence has been approved enjoy your trip to Europe.

12. Our two four and six hour seminars are competitively priced programs that have become very well known.

13. The candidate was quoted as saying, I will reduce government spending by 15 percent.

14. The latest issue of Chief Executive Officer contains an article on ethics.

15. This months issue will feature the first of a three part series on investing.

16. Since the last issue of the corporate directory was published there have been many changes offices have relocated managers have shifted.

17. Lombard Street the crookedest street in the world is in San Francisco California.

18. Remember Miss Barbeaux that this organization has two objectives service and productivity.

19. Rinji will be away from the office October 12 16.

20. The custodian said that the floors were waxed in November but the records show they have not been done since August.

Internal Punctuation

The exercises in the textbook and those you have just completed in this supplement have been designed to give you practice in inserting various punctuation marks. Remember, however, that not all sentences have internal punctuation. Keep that thought in mind as you insert punctuation in the following business messages.

1. Dear Publisher:

    Thank you for the time and effort you put into publishing <u>Business</u>. I have been a loyal reader for over three years and have enjoyed each issue. Now I would like to share the information contained in <u>Business</u> with my students. May I therefore have your permission to reprint the articles contained in your periodical and distribute them to the students enrolled in my Introduction to Business class.

    Several factors influence this request. First <u>Business</u> covers a wide variety of relevant topics. Second its concise easy to read articles will appeal to students. Finally the extensive use of graphics makes the articles well suited to the classroom environment.

Since I would like to begin using the articles next term I would appreciate your completing and returning the enclosed permission card within the next three weeks. You may be sure that each reprint will contain a complete citation listing <u>Business</u> as its source. I am confident that this exposure to <u>Business</u> will make my students avid readers of the publication.

Sincerely,

Susan Bates-Reuter

Susan Bates-Reuter

Enclosure

2. Dear Ms. Bates-Reuter:

Yes! You may have our permission to reprint articles contained in <u>Business</u> and distribute them to your students.

Please be sure that a citation including the name of the article the name of the publication the volume the issue number and the page number(s) appears on each reprint.

In order to encourage tomorrows business leaders to subscribe to <u>Business</u> today we offer a special subscription rate for students. A packet of brochures describing <u>Business</u> and the special student rate is enclosed. Please distribute the materials to your students and encourage them to subscribe.

We appreciate the comments you made about <u>Business</u> Ms. Bates-Reuter and are confident your students will be equally impressed by its thorough timely articles. If there is any other way in which we can be of help to you please let us know.

Yours truly,

3. TO: Joshua J. Goldstein

   FROM: R. M. Martinez   *R. M. M.*

   DATE: August 15, 199-

   SUBJECT: Annual Report

Congratulations! The annual report is exceptional. You and your staff spent a tremendous amount of time gathering the data designing the layout and doing the graphics. The results are definitely worth the effort.

Josh the Board of Directors was extremely pleased with the report and believes you and your staff deserve recognition both external and internal for your work. Therefore they have directed me to enter this years report in the contest sponsored by the Tri-State Public Relations Council and to arrange a reception to honor you and the members of your department. I will phone you next week to gather information for the award application and to discuss plans for the reception.

Thank you for a job well done.

WORD PUZZLE

Unscramble the letters below to form words related to punctuation.

1. mscieooln   ___________________________

2. snnsoentelia tslenmee   ___________________________

3. autqonoti krasm   ___________________________

4. enphyh   ___________________________

5. ohpaortsep   ___________________________

6. arpcnelehttai nxrsseipoe   ___________________________

7. slipsiel npotis   ___________________________

8. rtehnapsese   ___________________________

9. oqsnutei rakm   ___________________________

10. caeledarivt necsteen   ___________________________

CHAPTER 9

Style

LEARNING ACTIVITIES

True or False?

Circle T if the statement is true; circle F if the statement is false.

T　　F　　**1.** The *general style* for writing numbers blends two styles known as formal and informal.

T　　F　　**2.** Word division is an option, not a requirement.

T　　F　　**3.** Abbreviations are effective only when the reader of the message understands them.

T　　F　　**4.** The abbreviation used to represent times before noon is *p.m.*

T　　F　　**5.** Occupational titles should be capitalized only when they are also titles of specific jobs.

T　　F　　**6.** Word processing software makes it impossible for writers to choose to hyphenate words.

T　　F　　**7.** Figures should be used with percentages even when beginning a sentence.

T　　F　　**8.** Compass directions should be capitalized only if personified or part of a specific title.

T　　F　　**9.** In business correspondence, ".00" should be used with whole number money amounts.

T　　F　　**10.** Ordinal numbers show position in a series.

T　　F　　**11.** When a writer wishes to emphasize a time, a figure should be used before the word *o'clock.*

T　　F　　**12.** Follow the style on an organization's stationery for correct capitalization.

T　　F　　**13.** In most business writing, measurements are spelled out rather than abbreviated.

T   F   **14.** Months and days can be abbreviated in business correspondence as well as on forms.

T   F   **15.** In business writing, abbreviate a person's name only when you are sure the individual will not be offended.

Completion

Complete each sentence by writing the necessary word or words in the blanks.

1. Style governs the way we work with ________________________, ________________________, ________________________, and ________________________.

2. The two ways to display a number in business correspondence are as a/an ________________________ or as a/an ________________________.

3. Round numbers may be expressed as ________________________, ________________________, or ________________________.

4. A/An ________________________ is usually used in numbers of four or more digits.

5. The ordinal number for the word *second* is ________________________.

6. The house number in an address used as part of the text of a message should be expressed as a/an ________________________ if it is greater than ________________________.

7. A ________________________ is placed between house and street numbers expressed as figures when they are adjacent to one another.

8. ________________________ numbers are used when a day is used without a month or when the day precedes the month.

9. Fractions are displayed as ________________________ when they are part of ________________________.

10. ________________________ amounts of money are expressed as words.

11. The only general subject areas that should be capitalized are ________________________.

12. Capitalize the short forms of ________________________ and ________________________ government bodies and their major divisions.

13. Time can be a reference to not only a date but also a/an ________________________, a/an ________________________, or a/an ________________________.

14. Two resources helpful to writers who wish to divide words are a/an ________________________ and a/an ________________________.

15. ________________________ are abbreviations that are pronounced as words.

Matching

Write the letter of the abbreviation in the blank preceding the term. Some abbreviations may be used more than once; others may not be used at all.

__________	**1.** ampersand	**a.**	Ms.
__________	**2.** Company	**b.**	Wm.
__________	**3.** Mrs. or Miss	**c.**	Inc.
__________	**4.** asterisk	**d.**	#
__________	**5.** Robert	**e.**	Bill
__________	**6.** at, per, each	**f.**	Co.
__________	**7.** pounds	**g.**	*
__________	**8.** Incorporated	**h.**	T
__________	**9.** William	**i.**	@
__________	**10.** thousand	**j.**	"
__________	**11.** before noon	**k.**	Chas.
__________	**12.** Charles	**l.**	K
__________	**13.** number	**m.**	Mssr.
__________	**14.** Corporation	**n.**	'
__________	**15.** feet	**o.**	p.m.
		p.	Robt.
		q.	Chuck
		r.	a.m.
		s.	Corp.
		t.	Assn.
		u.	&

Fill-in-the-Blanks

Write the abbreviation for the term at the left in the blank at the right.

1. Lines per minute   __________

2. Northwest   __________

3. Registered Nurse   __________

4. Master of Fine Arts   __________

5. Characters per second   __________

6. Millimeter   __________

7. Acquired Immune Deficiency Syndrome   __________

8. Federal Bureau of Investigation   __________

9. United Nations   __________

10. American Association of Retired Persons   __________

WORD PUZZLE

Locate and circle the style-related words listed below. They may appear vertically, horizontally, or diagonally. Letters may be part of more than one word.

s	i	s	p	u	n	e	f	r	a	c	t	i	o	n	s
n	y	v	g	e	s	y	o	n	l	e	r	c	s	t	i
o	p	m	e	a	r	l	a	r	l	n	d	p	a	i	d
g	s	m	b	s	c	o	m	p	a	s	s	l	o	m	i
r	e	o	v	o	e	r	a	l	n	t	i	l	n	e	v
c	o	n	g	e	l	d	d	e	g	r	e	e	s	m	e
o	s	e	e	f	r	i	v	e	u	o	c	o	s	y	o
p	s	y	e	r	p	n	s	e	a	s	o	n	a	p	m
e	g	e	d	f	a	a	n	g	g	i	v	i	d	i	n
r	a	c	o	n	s	l	t	d	e	y	t	l	a	r	e
c	e	n	t	c	o	n	s	i	s	t	e	n	c	y	c
e	s	o	n	t	l	m	b	t	s	u	a	m	p	s	o
n	e	r	s	a	c	t	o	d	y	p	n	b	o	b	a
t	r	t	e	s	g	e	t	o	t	l	e	t	l	y	f
i	t	f	y	s	r	d	i	v	i	d	e	i	a	m	t
t	v	d	i	n	e	y	e	e	s	e	a	g	e	s	t

money	assn	fractions
general style	ordinal	symbol
compass	consistency	languages
percent	divide	season
time	degrees	ft

APPLICATION EXERCISES

1. List two ways in which you might use numbers to identify yourself in each of the following settings:

   a. School ____
   ____

   b. Work ____
   ____

   c. Home ____
   ____

2. Assume that a friend has given you the following draft of a letter and has asked you to check it for accuracy of number display, capitalization, and use of abbreviations. Locate and correct all the errors.

15 Aug. 199-

MS Maria Rodrigez
Smith and Varney
Twenty-seven Oak Ridge Place
Muncie, Indiana 47306-7648

Dear Ms Rodrigez

Thank you for your interest in the origin of the Postal ZIP Code and its recent expansion. It is a pleasure to furnish the following explanation.

The 5-digit ZIP Code was introduced to the public on July first, 1963. ZIP is an acronym for Zone Improvement Plan. The Plan was designed to speed the sorting and distribution of an ever-increasing volume of mail to a growing number of delivery points. The System has since been used as a logical method of geographic division & has been applied in many varied situations.

The first digit of the ZIP Code divides the country into 10 large groups of States numbered from 0 in the Northeast to 9 in the Far west. Within these areas, each state is divided into an average of 10 smaller areas. Each of these areas is identified by the 2nd and third digits of the ZIP Code. The last 2 digits identify a local delivery area.

The expanded system, called "ZIP + 4," has helped to keep Postage Rates down and to improve service. Street blocks, office buildings, and companies receiving large volumes of mail have been assigned a 4-digit add-on number. This number enables automatic sorting of mail all the way down to a particular segment of a carrier's route. The key to savings with the add-on digits has been in the use of optical character readers (O.C.R.s) that read the ZIP Code and process the item automatically.

The encl. brochures furnish addl. info. about the code. If you have any further questions about the use of the ZIP Code, Miss Rodrigez, please write me or call your local PO and speak with one of the Customer Service Representatives there.

Sincerely

(Mrs.) Jennifer p. Hammond
Regional Representative

lr

Enclosures

3. Refer to the title page of this workbook. Answer the following questions about the authors.

    a. Which author has a nickname? _______________________________

       What is it? _______________________________

    b. Which author might be better known to his/her friends by a shortened form of his/her name?

       ____

       What is one shortened form his/her given name might take? _______________________________

4. Complete the chart below by indicating syllabication and preferred division points for each word. Place a dot (.) between each syllable and a hyphen (-) at the preferred division point(s).

Word	Syllabication	Division Point(s)
Example: around	a. round	do not divide
a. frequently		
b. coordinate		
c. speaker		
d. calendar		
e. liability		
f. entitled		
g. prorated		
h. enclosure		
i. total		
j. intersect		
k. erase		
l. resident		
m. disaster		
n. popular		
o. expansion		

Formats of Letters and Memos

LEARNING ACTIVITIES

True or False?

Circle T if the statement is true; circle F if the statement is false.

T F **1.** A letterhead on business stationery may be printed using several colors.

T F **2.** Any color stationery is appropriate for all organizations.

T F **3.** The attention line is part of the letter address.

T F **4.** The company name may be included in the signature block when a letter is used in lieu of a contract.

T F **5.** Simplified memos should NOT be prepared on letterhead stationery.

T F **6.** The body of a memo is usually formatted in modified block style.

T F **7.** The number of enclosures may be included in the enclosure notation of a business letter.

T F **8.** A letter in simplified block format uses a salutation but eliminates the complimentary close.

T F **9.** A personal business letter does NOT require a specific format, but standard parts are the same as in a business letter.

T F **10.** The signature block of a business letter may include a courtesy title (Dr., Mr., or Mrs.).

Multiple Choice

Write the letter that represents the best answer in the blank at the left.

 **1.** Which of the following is NOT a standard part of a business letter?
   a. Salutation
   b. Signature block
   c. Enclosure notation
   d. Reference initials

 **2.** Your return address on a personal business letter should be
   a. printed within the top one inch of the stationery.
   b. omitted since it will be in the letterhead.
   c. centered at the top of the stationery.
   d. keyed immediately above the dateline or under the signature block.

 **3.** Which of the following is NOT a characteristic of a memo?
   a. Formal writing style is used
   b. Memo may be keyed in the top portion of the page
   c. Order of the memo heading may vary
   d. Body of memo is usually in block style

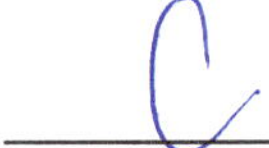 **4.** Which of the following is NOT a commonly used letter format?
   a. Block
   b. Mixed block
   c. Modified block
   d. Simplified block

5. The Postal Service recommends
   a. using all capital letters in the envelope address.
   b. using ZIP + 4 only for letters being sent to business organizations.
   c. keying instructions for individuals handling the receiver's mail in the lower right-hand corner of the envelope.
   d. using no more than one envelope notation on a single envelope.

Matching

Write the letter of the best answer in the blank preceding the description. Some answers may be used more than once; others may not be used at all.

_____ h, _____ 1. Greeting of letter

_____ m. _____ 2. Summarizes letter content

_____ m. _____ 3. Used for internal communication

_____ i. _____ 4. Contains position title of sender

_____ k. _____ 5. Multiform paper with heading and message portion

_____ n. _____ 6. Comma after salutation

_____ B. _____ 7. Upper left corner of envelope

_____ f. _____ 8. Lists persons to receive letter

_____ D. _____ 9. Most common business letter stationery

_____ c. _____ 10. Envelope notation

a. 20-pound bond

b. return address

c. Registered

d. simplified block

e. open punctuation

f. copy notation

g. memo heading

h. salutation

i. signature block

j. subject line

k. round-trip memo

l. modified block

m. memo

n. mixed punctuation

Completion

Complete each item by writing the necessary word or words.

1. The three parts of an envelope are _____return address_____, _____mailing address_____, and _____envelope notations_____.

2. Headings of formal memos are labeled _____To:_____, _____From:_____, _____Date:_____, and _____Subject:_____.

3. The letter format in which the body of the letter may contain indented paragraphs is _____modified block_____.

4. In a letter using the simplified block style, the _____salutation_____ is keyed a double space below the letter address.

5. A round-trip memo is also called a _____message-reply memo_____

6. The two standard parts of a letter that are omitted when simplified block format is used are _____salutation_____ and _____complimentary close_____

7. Reference initials include the initials of the _____originator_____ and may include the initials of the _____keyboard operator_____.

8. Personal business letters never contain _____reference initials_____, but business letters always contain them.

9. Envelope notations for individuals handling the receiver's mail are _____Confidential_____, _____hold for arrival_____, and _____please forward_____.

10. The heading of a business letter consists of the _____letterhead_____ and the _____dateline_____.

Review Questions

1. Compare block format of business letters with modified block format.

2. What is a letterhead and how can it affect the outcome of your business message?

3. Discuss the three parts that may be keyed on an envelope.

4. Compare formatting of personal business letters to formatting of business letters sent by organizations.

5. How do the expectations of your message receiver influence the message format and stationery that you choose?

APPLICATION EXERCISES

1. Find a business letter written in modified block form. Reformat the letter in simplified block form.

2. Write a letter to your instructor explaining when to use a letter and when to use a memo for internal communication. You may use any acceptable letter format.

3. Obtain letterhead stationery from an executive in a financial institution and paper used for advertisements from a service company. Compare the two pieces of paper.

4. Assume that you have just established your own company. Design a letterhead for this company, and explain how it depicts the image of the company.

5. Use a ZIP Code directory (post office or library) to get the correct ZIP Codes for the following locations:

   Raccoon, Kentucky
   Midland National Bank, Billings, Montana
   Cat Spring, Texas
   John F. Kennedy Federal Building, Boston, Massachusetts
   Floyds Knobs, Indiana
   Hope, Arkansas
   Yazoo City, Mississippi
   Puerto Real, Puerto Rico

6. You want more information about a camcorder that you saw advertised in a magazine. Reformat the following request letter using block, modified block, and simplified block formats. The company is PowerView Cameras in Dallas, Texas 75222-4431. It is located at 5217 King Ridge Avenue. Add any details to make this a complete letter. The body of the letter is:

   Please send me information about the PowerView VHS Camcorder. It was advertised in the April issue of *The Photographer*.

   I am enclosing a self-addressed, stamped envelope.

7. Write a formal memo to your instructor explaining your immediate and long-range goals after graduation. Pay particular attention to format and grammar.

WORD PUZZLE

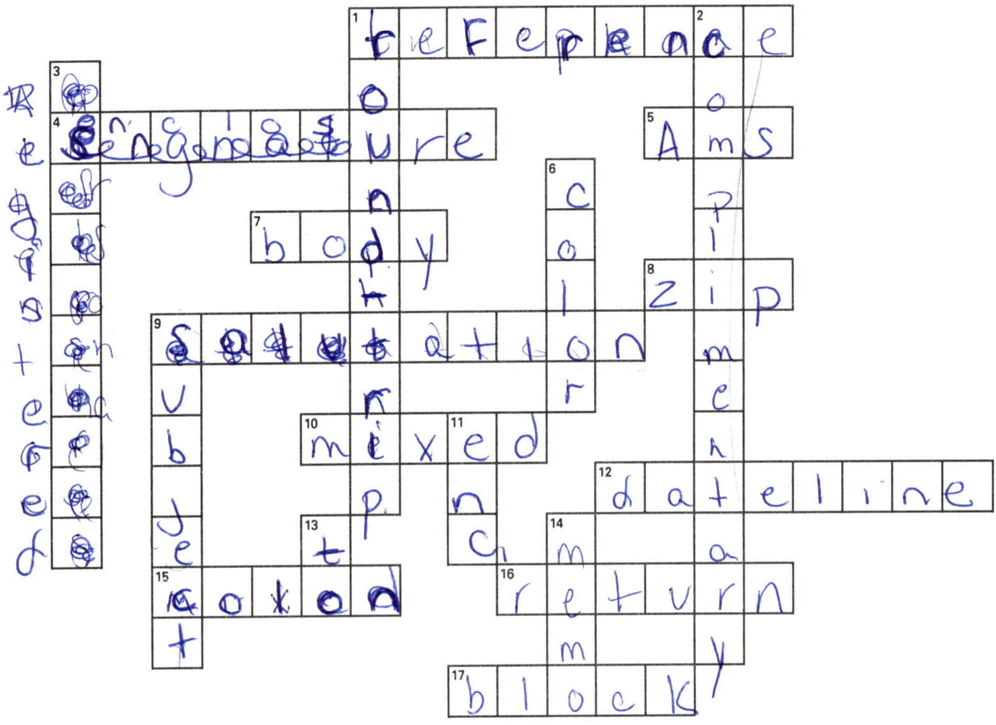

Across

1. _________ initials
4. Anything included with letter
5. Developed original simplified format
7. Letter message
8. Code used in addresses
9. Letter greeting
10. Punctuation style
12. Part of letter heading
15. Punctuation after salutation
16. Sender's address on envelope
17. A letter format

Down

1. Special form of memo
2. _________ close
3. Envelope notation
6. Consideration in selecting stationery
9. _________ line
11. Placed below reference initials (abbr.)
13. One part of memo heading
14. Used for internal communication

CHAPTER 11

Positive and Neutral Messages

LEARNING ACTIVITIES

True or False?

Circle T if the statement is true; circle F if the statement is false.

T   F   **1.** The positive information should always be placed in the opening of an adjustment approval.

T   F   **2.** Even though a claim letter may contain negative information, the writer should present the message positively.

T   F   **3.** Persuasion may be needed in some inquiries about products.

T   F   **4.** One important advantage of using the direct plan for positive or neutral messages is that it gets the receiver in the proper frame of mind.

T   F   **5.** The main idea of a message normally should follow the explanation of the positive or neutral information.

T   F   **6.** Questions in inquiries should be general in order to allow the respondent flexibility in answering.

T   F   **7.** In an adjustment message, the best place for an apology is in the close to help the receiver remember it.

T   F   **8.** Preferably, the positive and neutral message opening is presented in one compound or complex sentence.

T   F   **9.** Not all positive messages should be organized by using the direct plan.

T   F   **10.** Confidentiality of information is a necessity with some inquiries.

Multiple Choice

Write the letter that represents the best answer in the blank at the left.

__________ **1.** Positive information is emphasized most by
    a. a single-sentence paragraph near the middle of the letter.
    b. a single-sentence paragraph at the beginning of the letter.
    c. a two-sentence paragraph at the beginning of the letter.
    d. a two-sentence paragraph at the end of the letter.

__________ **2.** Which of the following is NOT considered an appropriate subject for an inquiry message?
    a. Individuals
    b. Complaints
    c. Products
    d. Services

__________ **3.** A writer's anger in a claim letter should be
    a. emphasized.
    b. suggested.
    c. implied.
    d. suppressed.

__________ **4.** Which is NOT a characteristic of a positive information opening in a direct plan?
    a. Stresses writer's interests
    b. Is positive
    c. Provides related explanation
    d. Uses emphasis techniques

__________ **5.** Which statement would be the most appropriate close for an adjustment message?
    a. We regret the inconvenience that this has caused you.
    b. Hopefully, our corrective action will keep this situation from happening again.
    c. Best wishes on your store expansion.
    d. This problem will never reoccur.

Matching

Write the letter of the best answer in the blank preceding the term. Some answers may be used more than once; others may not be used at all.

__________ 1. Announcement of an unscheduled pay increase

__________ 2. Claim letter

__________ 3. Content development

__________ 4. Direct plan

__________ 5. Explanation

__________ 6. Friendly close

__________ 7. Inquiry

__________ 8. Opening

__________ 9. Request approvals

__________ 10. Sales appeal

a. expresses appreciation

b. you–viewpoint

c. use only when appropriate

d. presents related information

e. letter of appreciation

f. done after situation is analyzed

g. used for positive and neutral messages

h. normally given

i. should de-emphasize the inconvenience that sender has experienced

j. appears before the explanation

k. used to obtain information

l. type of unsolicited positive message

Completion

Complete each item by writing the necessary word or words.

1. A well-constructed explanation should stress the benefits to the ______________________ instead of the interests of the ______________________.

2. Positive and neutral messages should be organized by using the ______________________ plan.

3. A direct plan should be used for messages presenting ______________________, ______________________, or ______________________.

4. The sales appeal, if appropriate, should follow the ______________________.

5. An effectively written positive or neutral message integrates ______________________ ______________________ into the direct plan.

6. Immediate information is provided to the receiver by identifying the order or request in the
   _______________________ paragraph or a _______________________ line.

7. The direct plan begins by presenting _______________________.

8. An individual's rights may be protected in an inquiry when _______________________
   and _______________________.

9. Adjustments to claims should be made _______________________.

10. The content of the message is developed using the direct plan after the _______________________
    and _______________________.

Review Questions

1. What is an adjustment message? How is its content organized?

2. How can the you–viewpoint be implemented in a positive information message?

3. Explain the differences between writing a positive information message to an employee and
   writing a positive information message to a customer.

4. What must take place in the message development process before the content is developed?

5. Explain why the following paragraph would be weak in opening an inquiry message.

   Your company has an excellent reputation in the business community. Your products are
   being used throughout the United States.

CASE PROBLEMS

Inquiries

1. Twelve employees of Brenham National Bank will be in Dallas, Texas, from May 29 to June 2.
   They have expressed an interest in either arriving one day early or leaving one day late so that
   they may attend the LaCosta Dinner Theater. You have been selected by the group to plan this
   activity. Write a letter to LaCosta to obtain details. Supply necessary information to make it a
   complete letter.

2. Carefree Insurance is concerned about the physical condition of its employees. After surveying
   the employees, it was decided that providing a racquetball court would be the best facility for
   getting its employees into shape. You have been assigned to gather information about constructing a racquetball court. Write a letter to Sports Freaks, Inc., to obtain this information. You will
   need enough information for management to make a decision.

3. You would like to put vinyl siding on your home, and you are considering installing it yourself. You need information such as cost, available styles and colors, installation procedures, and warranty. Write a letter to Quality All-Season Siding to obtain this information. Supply necessary information to make it a complete letter.

Requests

4. This past spring your organization constructed a Wellness Center for use by all employees. After the Center was in operation for several weeks, the employees requested that their lunch hour be extended to 1 1/2 hours to allow for more time to exercise, to shower, and to eat a quick lunch. You, as director of Human Resources, realize the benefits that the employees are gaining from the Center. After conferring with top management, you write a memo to all employees informing them that they can take a 1 1/2 hour lunch break to use the Wellness Center, but will have to make up the extra half-hour either before or after work.

5. You are the owner of Useful Robotics. Your organization manufactures robots that are sold or leased to business firms to perform repetitive and monotonous chores.

   The Forney Community Theater is presenting a comedy in which a robot is used. The director of the theater has requested that your organization donate the use of a robot. The theater group has a very limited budget and cannot afford to buy or lease one.

   Prepare a letter to the director, Ms. Amy Ragan, and tell her that a robot will be provided. This gesture will give your company much-needed publicity for its product. Be sure to include any necessary details to make this a complete request approval.

6. Because of your business education background, a local church has asked you to audit its books for the past year. The set of books is small and will not take too much time.

   Write Reverend Jim Wright a letter accepting this responsibility. In this letter you need to establish a date when you could meet with the church treasurer to go over the books.

Claims

7. You ordered a food processor from Kitchen Accessories after seeing one demonstrated on television. Unfortunately, the processor does not work nearly as well as the one demonstrated on television. The first time you sliced vegetables with it, the blade bent. Write Kitchen Accessories asking for a full refund. Add the necessary facts to make your letter complete.

8. Steven Erwin has always been overweight. He recently went to Pounds Away Camp to lose weight. This camp is especially designed for individuals who want to lose weight while vacationing.

   After two weeks at the camp Steven gained four pounds instead of losing weight. When Steven returned home, he remembered that the camp guaranteed a weight loss.

   Write a letter for Steven requesting a refund of $1,800 (the cost of his camping vacation). Indicate that a copy of the brochure advertising the guaranteed weight loss is included.

9. Pat Freeman's home on the edge of town looks beautiful, with four large young trees in the front yard. The trees were 15 feet tall when planted last fall. Westrup's Nursery did an excellent landscaping job with the trees.

   Pat is unhappy now after a winter snowstorm broke three of the main limbs from one of the trees. Write a letter for Pat to Westrup's Nursery and ask for a $575 refund or a replacement tree. The storm was not so severe that the trees should have been damaged.

Adjustments

10. The Pounds Away Camp is operated for people who would like to lose weight while vacationing. You have been operating this camp for six years and have seen hundreds of people lose weight. Because of this experience, you began issuing guarantees that would give any person who did not successfully lose some weight a full refund.

    Steven Erwin stayed at the camp for two weeks and gained four pounds. Although it was rumored that Steven was snacking at night (which is against the rules), your staff did not catch him. Because you have a reputation to maintain, you will give him a full refund of $1,800. Write him a letter approving the adjustment; enclose the check.

11. You operate Fantasia Ceiling Fans, a mail-order business. Priscilla Young of Jackson, Mississippi, purchased a 60-inch, contemporary ceiling fan from you this past summer. You have just received a letter from her stating:

    > I purchased a 60-inch, limited edition, polished brass fan with four white blades in late June. Your advertisement stated that it was constructed of sturdy, die-cast zinc and steel. It contained a 3-speed reversible fan motor.
    >
    > The fan was installed by a licensed electrician the first week in July. During Labor Day weekend I heard an unusual sound when I turned on the fan. Over the next two weeks as I was using the fan, the noise seemed to get worse. Now the fan is vibrating whenever I turn it on. I wish you would send me a new fan or refund my money.

    Write Ms. Young a letter explaining that you will send her a new fan. In this letter tell her that apparently the motor is malfunctioning. Inform her that the new fan will have the same warranty as the original fan. Add necessary details.

12. Ralph Teague is the customer service representative for Alvarado Electronics, a manufacturer of sound and video equipment. Equipment manufactured by Alvarado Electronics is sold in retail stores throughout the United States.

    Jane Mayfield has written a letter to Ralph stating that she purchased one of Alvarado's tape recorders 14 months ago from a local discount store. The recorder was guaranteed for one year. She would like a replacement unit since the warranty had so recently expired.

    Write a letter for Mr. Teague telling Ms. Mayfield that she can return the tape recorder to any store that sells Alvarado products. The letter should explain that the store is to give Ms. Mayfield a replacement unit and then forward the defective recorder to Alvarado Electronics for reimbursement.

Unsolicited Positive and Neutral Messages

13. Champion Savings has expanded its facilities during remodeling. It added an activity room that can be used for various functions, such as bridal showers, birthday parties, anniversaries, receptions, etc. The room is available to any of Champion's patrons who have both checking and savings accounts with the institution. Write a form letter that could be sent to all of Champion Savings customers.

14. As vice-president of advertising for Safety Tire Company you are aware of the advantages of high-volume sales. To achieve these high-volume sales, you realize that rewards must be given to retailers.

    A program has been developed by Safety Tire Company that will give the retailer a rebate of $35 for every ten tires sold during a six-month promotional period. Write a letter informing the retailers of this promotional plan. Add the necessary facts to make your letter complete.

15. Yuki Yamaguchi has been working as an information processing operator for Cummins Insurance for the past three months and has developed excellent work skills.

    You are the human resources manager for Cummins. Write a memo to Yuki promoting her to supervisor of the Information Processing Service Center. Explain to her that you normally do not promote anyone in your organization that quickly, but you are doing so in this situation because of her outstanding performance.

CHAPTER 12

Negative Messages

LEARNING ACTIVITIES

True or False?

Circle T if the statement is true; circle F if the statement is false.

T   F   **1.** The indirect plan should be used for all negative messages.

T   F   **2.** An advantage of using the indirect plan for negative messages is that after giving the negative information, the logical explanation is presented and offsets the message's negative impact.

T   F   **3.** It is possible that the presentation of a negative message can show the receiver that the negative information is, in fact, in his or her best interest.

T   F   **4.** In the opening buffer of a negative message, the sender tries to maintain neutrality and not imply either a yes or a no.

T   F   **5.** The logical explanation section of a negative message contains a helpful alternative solution.

T   F   **6.** The logical explanation justifies the negative information.

T   F   **7.** Giving the negative information positively means avoiding negative words and saying what can be done rather than what cannot.

T   F   **8.** If appropriate, you can give an additional reason in the constructive follow-up justifying the unfavorable news.

T   F   **9.** The off-the-subject close should contain a sincere apology to help build goodwill with the receiver.

T   F   **10.** Any message that is unpleasant, disappointing, or unfavorable in the mind of the receiver is considered a negative message.

Matching

Write the letter of the appropriate part of the indirect plan for negative messages that contains the requirement listed.

__________ **1.** Introduces the explanation

__________ **2.** Provides alternative solution

__________ **3.** Presents convincing reasoning

__________ **4.** Says what can be done (not what cannot)

__________ **5.** Stresses receiver interests and benefits

__________ **6.** Maintains neutrality

__________ **7.** Telegraphs explanation

__________ **8.** Stays off negative subject

__________ **9.** Follows logical explanation

__________ **10.** Follows opening

a. The opening buffer

b. The logical explanation

c. The negative information

d. The constructive follow-up

e. The friendly close

Multiple Choice

Write the letter that represents the best answer in the blank at the left.

__________ **1.** The overall strategy for most negative messages is
 a. the direct plan.
 b. the persuasive plan.
 c. the indirect plan.
 d. the goodwill plan.

__________ **2.** An important requirement of the opening buffer in the indirect plan is that it
 a. presents convincing reasoning.
 b. provides coherence.
 c. follows the logical explanation.
 d. says what can be done.

__________ **3.** One of the most important requirements of the logical explanation is that it
 a. provides an alternative solution.
 b. stays off the negative subject.
 c. uses emphasis techniques.
 d. maintains neutrality.

_________ **4.** If you cannot provide an alternative solution in a negative message, you are encouraged in the constructive follow-up to
  a. give additional reasoning.
  b. be positive.
  c. personalize it.
  d. be optimistic.

_________ **5.** The negative information in a message should
  a. be given quickly.
  b. follow the opening.
  c. present convincing reasoning.
  d. introduce the explanation.

_________ **6.** When closing a negative message, it is important to
  a. give additional reasoning.
  b. avoid referring to the negative information.
  c. imply the negative information.
  d. follow the logical explanation.

_________ **7.** The direct plan should be used for negative information when
  a. goodwill is important.
  b. the receiver should read the logical explanation first.
  c. an apology is important.
  d. your receiver prefers that the negative information be given first.

_________ **8.** Which of the following statements is not an advantage of the indirect plan?
  a. It emphasizes the negative information.
  b. It permits reason to prevail.
  c. It changes a negative situation to a positive one.
  d. It maintains a calm approach.

_________ **9.** Of the following, which is the most effective phrasing for negative information?
  a. I am sorry to refuse your request for a refund for the microwave oven.
  b. Our policy does not permit refunds in cases like this.
  c. Rather than a refund, we will be glad to provide instruction on the operation of the oven.
  d. While we realize you are not completely satisfied with the microwave oven, we do believe that you can be with additional training.

_________ **10.** The best opening for an adjustment refusal is
  a. I am sorry . . .
  b. Your complaint has been received, and . . .
  c. Thank you for your letter of . . .
  d. Your letter requesting an adjustment has been received, and . . .

WORD PUZZLE

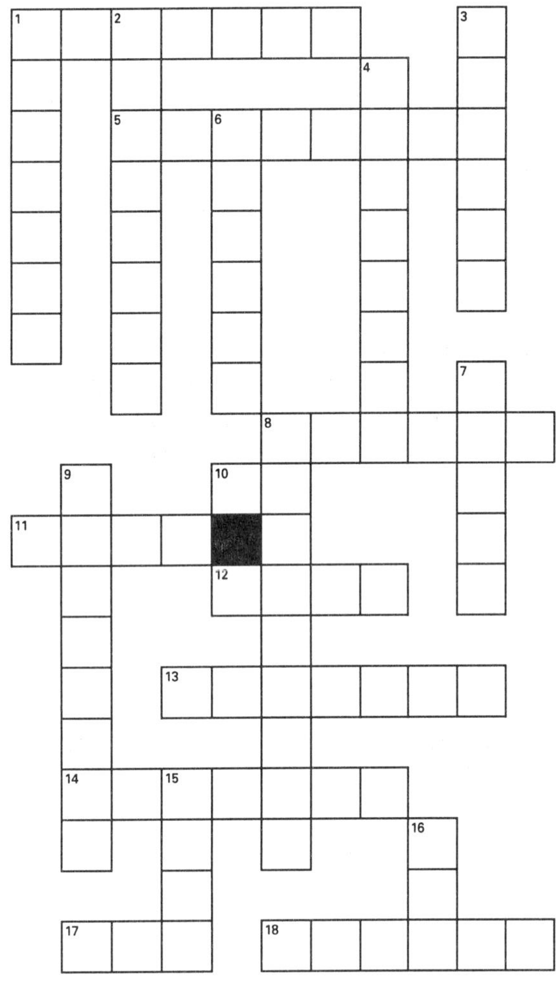

Across

1. Request _________

5. Good plan for negative messages

8. _________ refusal message

10. Common negative word

11. Letter that handles a large number of refusals

12. Negative information is bad _____ to receiver

13. Buffer

14. Nature of the explanation

17. Information that needs to be de-emphasized

18. Opening _________

Down

1. _________ refusal

2. _________ close

3. _________ goodwill

4. Avoid these words

6. Use this plan when appropriate

7. Give negative information _________ in direct plan

8. Same wave length

9. Important to maintain

15. The opposite of bad

16. _________-the-subject closing

CASE PROBLEMS

Request Refusals

1. Write a request refusal letter to the chair of the nominating committee of your community service club who has asked that you serve as president next year. You have been a member of the club for five years, and you think its purposes are worthy, but you are not in a position now to take a leadership role. You simply do not have the time. You have just been promoted to supervisor and are working between 50 and 70 hours per week and see no change in your work requirements in the foreseeable future. Supply any additional details needed.

2. You manage a restaurant in the Shade-Tree Mall. You have a moderate amount of window space where you display a copy of your menu. Juan Ramirez, a local banker who is also chairperson of the mental health board, has written to you requesting permission to place a large placard in your window space. The placard is promoting a worthwhile cause—the annual Marathon for Mental Health. Your policy, however, is to display only your menu in the limited window space. Supplying any additional necessary details, write Mr. Ramirez giving him the negative information. It will be important to justify your policy in your letter.

3. One of the employees in your plant, Sandra Smith, is running for mayor of your city. If she wins the election, she will take a leave of absence to serve her term. You have agreed to this. Also, as is your policy, you have contributed $500 to each of the two candidates in the election. You believe in assisting all sides in getting their positions before the voting public. Ms. Smith has just sent you a memo requesting a second $500 contribution. In this request, as in her first request, she very persuasively points out that it will be in your company's interest that she win the election. Write her the necessary request refusal message. Show her how your policy is in her best interest and benefits her most. As a suggested alternative, you could offer permission to both candidates for them to solicit contributions through memos to the employees.

Adjustment Refusals

4. As adjustment manager of the retail mail-order company that sells "Young Jeans," you have received a challenging claim letter. David Robinson writes, "I have just laundered the jeans I purchased from you last week. They shrank, they faded, and they wrinkled! Send my $49.95 back today, and tell me what to do with the jeans." You must refuse his claim. All the things that he said happened undoubtedly did. In fact, the small brochure attached to each pair of these all-cotton jeans said they would. Write Mr. Robinson an adjustment refusal that will stress the qualities of "Young Jeans" that will serve him well. In fact, you will not only turn down his claim, but you will also try to sell him (in your suggested alternative) some "Just You Jeans" that will not shrink, fade, or wrinkle.

5. You manage Swimmers' Delight, a discount, mail-order bathing suit sales organization. Write a form letter to customers who are asking to return bathing suits purchased from your company. Your policy—stated clearly in your sales catalog—is not to allow the return of bathing suits for personal hygiene reasons. In all your catalogs you stress that customers should select sizes carefully. You provide a sizing chart and fabric samples to assist them in their suit selections. Be sure to justify your policy to your customers. Add any necessary details to make this a complete form letter that fully utilizes the indirect plan for negative messages.

6. Joanna Collins has just left your office. She is upset. The new car she purchased from your dealership is having carburetor problems. She has called you several times about the problem. She wants the problem corrected at no cost to her. Each time you have tried to explain patiently (a) that her warranty expired a month before the trouble began, and (b) that you can repair the carburetor if she will leave the car in your garage for two days. Joanna is so angry now she is threatening to sue. You believe she has no legal basis for her position, but you do not want to be sued or to lose any future business you might have with her. You feel the best thing to do at this point is to write her an adjustment refusal letter, clearly specifying the situation. You have also decided, as a suggested alternative, to offer to do the necessary repair at cost. Write the indirect letter that will restore Joanna's goodwill.

Credit Refusals

7. As credit manager for Hahn's, Inc., you review applications for store credit cards. Today's mail brought an application from a newly married male. He is requesting that he and his wife be extended a line of credit and that credit cards be issued to each. A check of their credit ratings reveals that he currently is in bankruptcy, but that her credit rating is good. Write a credit refusal to him, but try to keep his and his wife's business.

8. You are the credit manager for Rosewood Wholesale Electric in Chicago, Illinois. An application for credit has just been received from Parkdale Electric, Parkdale, Illinois, a relatively new cash customer. With the application, Parkdale provided all the necessary supporting references, none of which look good. Although Parkdale's cash purchases are getting larger each month (last month they were a gratifying $903), the references indicate a poor Dun and Bradstreet rating, a poor assets-to-liabilities ratio, and evidences of slow payment from the Chicago Credit Bureau report. Using the indirect plan, deny Parkdale Electric credit, but retain its business. In the near future Parkdale may qualify for credit with you; in the meantime, you definitely want its cash business. Add the facts necessary to make your letter complete in proper format.

9. Write a form letter that can be sent to older persons who have applied for your new "BuyFree" credit card but who do not meet your credit requirements. It is ironic that many of these older people are quite well off financially; but because they have always paid cash for their purchases, they have not established creditworthy records. Refuse to issue the credit card in so tactful a manner that you are sure to get their business when they take the necessary steps to establish their credit records. In fact, do more than is expected by telling them some of the steps they can take to establish a credit record—for example, borrowing a small amount from a bank and paying it back before it is due, buying an item on credit from a local retailer and paying promptly for it, etc. Add any necessary details.

Unsolicited Negative Messages

10. When you accepted your present position as manager of accounting services eight months ago, you thought you would stay in the position at least three years. But now you have had an excellent offer from a rival accounting firm to manage one of its branch offices. Not only will you have more responsibility, but you will also receive a significant increase in pay. It is a major advancement for you. You know, however, that your superior will be seriously disappointed, perhaps even angry, for she thought you would remain with the firm for at least another three to five years. Write an indirect plan letter that explains your decision. State the negative

information positively. In the suggested alternative section of the letter, speak of your assistant's ability to assume your position.

11. Write an unsolicited form letter to the students in a dormitory telling them that their old, favorite dorm is going to be razed at the end of the semester and that they will have to move to another dorm or to private housing. The dorm is no longer cost-effective to maintain and only marginally meets safety and health standards. In addition, a parking lot is desperately needed for student parking in the area where the old dorm is located. After your opening buffer and explanation, do more than is expected and tell them how your office will facilitate their selection of new housing and their move to it.

12. You have talked to Mary Cohoon on three separate occasions about her unsatisfactory performance as a salesperson for the Harrison Insurance Agency's Salina office. The situation is getting worse instead of better. You have decided that the only decision left is to let her go. She obviously does not have the aptitude for sales work. She, too, is very unhappy with her performance. She has tried hard to sell insurance, but has had limited success. Write Mary a compassionate, unsolicited negative memo in which you terminate her employment with the Harrison Insurance Agency. There are definite receiver benefits in this dismissal situation. An employer does a favor for unsatisfactory employees, at least in part, by dismissing them when their skills do not match the job requirements.

CHAPTER 13

Persuasive Messages

LEARNING ACTIVITIES

True or False?

Circle T if the statement is true; circle F if the statement is false.

T   F   **1.** Persuasive messages are used in both internal and external communication.

T   F   **2.** Persuasive messages normally should be presented using the indirect approach.

T   F   **3.** Mechanical devices, such as color, should not be used to gain the reader's attention in a persuasive message because they distract the reader.

T   F   **4.** Emphasizing benefits to the receiver will help diminish negative reactions that the receiver may have to taking the desired action.

T   F   **5.** Both simple and complex requests are used by business organizations.

T   F   **6.** Recommendations usually are organized using the indirect persuasive plan.

T   F   **7.** Often a salutation is omitted in a sales letter.

T   F   **8.** Sales letters are usually prepared for multiple receivers.

T   F   **9.** The appeal stage of collection messages is used for customers who simply forgot to make a payment.

T   F   **10.** The number of steps in each collection stage should be consistent from customer to customer to ensure unbiased treatment.

Multiple Choice

Write the letter that represents the best answer in the blank at the left.

__________ **1.** Which of the following is NOT a guide to be used in constructing the action section of persuasive messages?
   a. Be direct and positive
   b. Require little effort for receiver to take action
   c. Motivate the receiver to think about the message
   d. Be optimistic that receiver will take desired action

__________ **2.** Which of the following methods of getting the receiver to take action should NOT be used in persuasive requests or sales letters?
   a. Using threats
   b. Offering free prizes
   c. Offering coupons
   d. Giving a deadline

__________ **3.** The indirect plan should be used for
   a. routine claims.
   b. goodwill messages.
   c. recommendation letters.
   d. adjustment grant letters.

__________ **4.** Which of the following comments best describes a collection message in the appeal stage?
   a. Is a reminder for a customer who forgot to pay
   b. Uses the indirect persuasive outline
   c. Is written from the writer's point of view
   d. Is not concerned with customer goodwill

__________ **5.** Which of the following sentence beginnings best asks for action in a collection appeal stage?
   a. You must send . . .
   b. I appeal to you to . . .
   c. Please send . . .
   d. I expect your . . .

Matching

Write the letter of the best answer in the blank preceding the term. Some answers may be used more than once; others may not be used at all.

__________	1. Action section	**a.**	begins most persuasive messages
__________	2. Attention section	**b.**	ends most persuasive messages
__________	3. Desire section	**c.**	submitted on all organizational levels
__________	4. Interest section	**d.**	builds on attention
__________	5. Past due	**e.**	uses direct plan
__________	6. Collection messages	**f.**	written in three stages
__________	7. Recommendations	**g.**	organized using both direct and indirect plan
__________	8. Sales messages	**h.**	example of message in reminder stage
__________	9. Special claims	**i.**	provides proof of receiver's benefits
__________	10. Warning stage	**j.**	other than routine
		k.	frequently omits salutation

Completion

Complete each item by writing the necessary word or words.

1. The two primary purposes of a persuasive message are

   ____ and

   ____.

2. Messages that are considered persuasive are:

   a. ____

   b. ____

   c. ____

   d. ____

   e. ____

   f. ____

3. The final paragraph of a persuasive message is designed to get the reader to
    ____.

4. Describing _______________________________to the receiver will create interest in the
    receiver.

5. _______________________________are submitted at all organizational levels.

6. Special claims requiring persuasion should be written using the
    ____ plan.

7. As you compose a sales message, you should emphasize the _______________________________
    and omit mentioning _______________________________________.

8. The three stages of collection messages are _______________________, _______________________,
    and _______________________.

9. The customer needs to be analyzed carefully before a collection letter is written in the
    _______________________________stage.

10. The indirect plan is used for collection letters in the _______________________________ stage.

Review Questions

1. What advantage is gained by using the indirect plan instead of the direct plan for persuasive
    messages?

2. Explain the indirect plan that should be used for persuasive messages in business communica-
    tions. Include all parts of the plan in your explanation.

3. Compare the organizational plans for the two types of requests that an organization uses.

4. Identify five techniques that may be used in sales messages to gain the reader's attention.

5. Compare the appeal stage of collection messages to the warning stage.

CASE PROBLEMS

Persuasive Requests

1. Turner Properties owns a storage facility that rents spaces for short-term and long-term periods.
    Space may be rented on a monthly or annual basis. Turner Properties has decided to increase the
    rent beginning next month. The current and new rental fees are:

	Current		New	
	Monthly	**Annual**	**Monthly**	**Annual**
5′ × 5′	$9.50	$95.00	$11.50	$115.00
5′ × 10′	$18.00	$180.00	$23.00	$230.00
10′ × 10′	$35.00	$350.00	$47.00	$470.00
10′ × 20′	$70.00	$700.00	$95.00	$950.00

In addition to providing storage, the facility provides an on-site manager; security fence; garage-style, roll-up doors; and 24-hour availability. Prepare a form message that can be sent to current renters informing them of the rental increase and encouraging them to accept the increase. Add necessary details.

2. Jack Page has been an active supporter of several youth organizations in your community. Project Leadership has decided to honor Jack for his contribution by naming him recipient of this year's Citizen of the Year Award. As president of Project Leadership, it is your responsibility to get Jack to the banquet without letting him know that he is to receive the award. Add details to make the letter complete.

3. You are chairperson of the program committee for Westwood Sports Club. One of your college classmates, Pat Evans, was a member of the U.S. Olympic team and won a silver medal in marksmanship. You did not know her well but would like to invite her to your club to give a demonstration. Pat charges a fee for her demonstration, however, and your club has no money. Write her a letter persuading her to give this demonstration without charge. Add necessary facts to make the letter complete.

Recommendations

4. The bookstore at your school handles a limited line of clothing in addition to textbooks. The line of clothing that it carries is excellent quality, but it is very expensive. Write a letter to the bookstore manager recommending that the present items be replaced with more affordable clothes.

5. You are president of Students for Action (SFA). This organization supported the present governor during the recent election. SFA would now like Art Fowler, an alumnus of your college, to be appointed to the state education board. Art has maintained his interest in your school's activities and has been very successful in operating a hardware store since his graduation. He is active in three civic organizations. Art would be an excellent individual to have on the board. Write a letter to the governor recommending Art for the position. Add necessary details to make the letter complete.

6. You are the manager of a horse farm in Lexington, Kentucky. Angela Forrester has been your veterinarian for 10 years. She has done an excellent job with the horses on your farm. Angela would like to become the veterinarian for the Commonwealth of Kentucky. Write a letter to the governor recommending her for the position.

Special Claims

7. Jane Broach purchased a fur coat on sale from Helene's Furrier for $2,150. She has had the coat for only one year, and the fur has started falling out. Jane has asked you to write a letter to Helene's requesting either a refund or another coat. Write the letter adding any details to make the letter complete.

8. Last summer you purchased a new motor home that you plan to use during vacations, weekends, and holidays. You started noticing minor problems (loose seat braces, leaking faucets, leaking side windows, tears in the seams of three seats, and several rattles) in the motor home after you had owned it for only three months. On your last trip with the motor home, the engine sputtered for most of the trip. On your return, you took it to the repair shop, where you learned that the carburetor needs replacing. You are unhappy with the motor home and feel that it is a "lemon." Write to Hughes Homes, the manufacturer, asking for a replacement motor home. Add details to make the letter complete.

9. During a recent hailstorm, damage was done to the roof of your home. An adjustor awarded you full damages, less your $100 deductible. Two weeks later, your television had to be repaired. The repair service representative stated that the damage was due to lightning, and the only storm in the past month was the one that damaged your roof. Write a letter to the insurance company requesting that the $135 repair bill for the television be combined with the roof so that you do not have to pay the $100 deductible twice. Add any details to make the letter complete.

Sales Messages

10. You are the owner-manager of a sporting goods store that is sponsoring a fishing derby; proceeds will go to Abused Children. Registration fees (not tax deductible) for the event are $10. Ten prizes totaling $500 will be awarded. Write a letter to customers on your mailing list announcing this derby.

11. Harbor Hills Marine is a full-service boat company. Recently, it began selling jet skis for water-sport recreation. The jet skis are similar to snowmobiles but are made to ride on water. They are dependable and provide the owner with years of fun and excitement. Prepare a sales message that could be sent to residents within the county. Add details to make the letter interesting and realistic.

12. Apple Motors is a sports car dealer. It has made arrangements with a local bank to finance all new cars sold to students who are within three months of graduation. Write a letter that could be sent to seniors notifying them of this arrangement.

Collection Messages

13. Fred's Photography specializes in wedding portraits. Fred's requires a $100 deposit and 25 percent of the balance when the pictures are delivered. The remaining balance can then be paid over a six-month period. Mark and Janet Slatta had a June wedding and received their pictures the first week of July, paying 25 percent at that time. However, they have not made a payment on the balance since getting the pictures. It is now November, and the balance is still $475.25. Fred's has written six collection letters without getting a response. Write a letter for Fred's

informing Mark and Janet that they have until December 1 to pay the $475.25 or the account will be given to an attorney. Add details to make the letter complete.

14. You deliver the local newspaper to earn money for school. The newspaper requires that carriers pay their bill for each month by the fifth of the following month. Alan Taylor, a subscriber, has not paid his bill for the last three months. You have enclosed four reminders with his paper, but they did not obtain a response. Write a letter to Alan appealing for the $22.50 due and explain why it is important that you collect his money each month. You do not want to antagonize Alan and lose him as a customer.

15. Northside Fitness Center is a diverse health facility. It provides its members with a full court gymnasium, outdoor pool and tennis courts, exercise classes, indoor running track, supervised weight training, racquetball courts, and child care during certain hours. A reminder sticker is pasted to overdue bills. Most members will respond to the reminders, but some members need more persuasion in order to pay their bills. Prepare a form letter that could be sent to members who are two or more months behind in their monthly dues. Add details to make the letter complete.

CHAPTER 14

Goodwill Messages

LEARNING ACTIVITIES

True or False?

Circle T if the statement is true; circle F if the statement is false.

T   F   **1.** The most important consideration for an appreciation letter is its length.

T   F   **2.** Sympathy messages should be written in the indirect approach because they deal with negative material.

T   F   **3.** Rarely should you use a handwritten message for a letter of condolence.

T   F   **4.** It is acceptable for an invitation to be printed on company stationery.

T   F   **5.** A goodwill message should cause the receiver to form a positive opinion of the sender.

T   F   **6.** A commercially printed greeting card is often used to convey goodwill for a holiday.

T   F   **7.** It is acceptable for the sender to write a personal note on a printed holiday greeting card sent by a company.

T   F   **8.** Goodwill messages are important in building positive relationships.

T   F   **9.** Welcome letters should not contain any coupons or sales offers.

T   F   **10.** Many communities have a professional organization whose purpose it is to welcome newcomers to the community.

Multiple Choice

Write the letter that represents the best answer in the blank at the left.

__________ 1. A formal, typewritten letter is most appropriate for
   a. a condolence letter.
   b. an invitation.
   c. a welcome letter.
   d. a holiday greeting.

__________ 2. Which of the following sentences would be the most appropriate for the closing paragraph in a condolence message?
   a. Best wishes in rebuilding your company.
   b. All of our employees join me in expressing our sympathy to you.
   c. You can be thankful that it wasn't worse.
   d. I am sorry that it had to happen to your organization.

__________ 3. An item that could be omitted from an invitation is
   a. date of function
   b. location of function
   c. RSVP
   d. signature

__________ 4. Which of the following is the best beginning sentence for a letter of appreciation?
   a. You have worked for our company for more than 35 years.
   b. You are invited to attend our annual banquet on August 22.
   c. Thank you for serving as a judge for the Outstanding Citizen of the Decade contest.
   d. We know that you will enjoy your retirement.

__________ 5. One consideration for the formality of a goodwill message is
   a. the amount of money you have to spend.
   b. how well you know the receiver.
   c. the importance of the message.
   d. the educational level of the receiver.

Completion

Complete each item by writing the necessary word or words.

1. Congratulatory messages should be written using the _____________________ approach.

2. The most personal and appreciated condolence messages are _____________________.

3. Messages of sympathy should be closed by _________________ _____________________.

4. Letters of appreciation may be sent for _____________________________ or for _____________________________.

5. Necessary details of an invitation include:

   a. ____

   b. ____

   c. ____

   d. ____

6. Some companies send distinctively designed holiday greeting cards that contain their
   ____________________________________ and ____________________________________.

7. A welcome message may be sent to ____________________________,
   ____________________________, or ____________________________.

8. A goodwill message is written to communicate ____________________________ and
   ____________________________.

9. A ____________________________ is a request for an individual's presence.

10. The most preferred method of accepting a new credit card customer is to send a
    ____________________________ letter.

Review Questions

1. Cite three situations that are appropriate for a letter of condolence.

2. Briefly discuss the composition of a condolence message.

3. Compare the contents of an invitation to the contents of a welcome message.

4. When is it appropriate to send each of the following forms of messages—handwritten, typewritten, or printed?

WORD PUZZLE

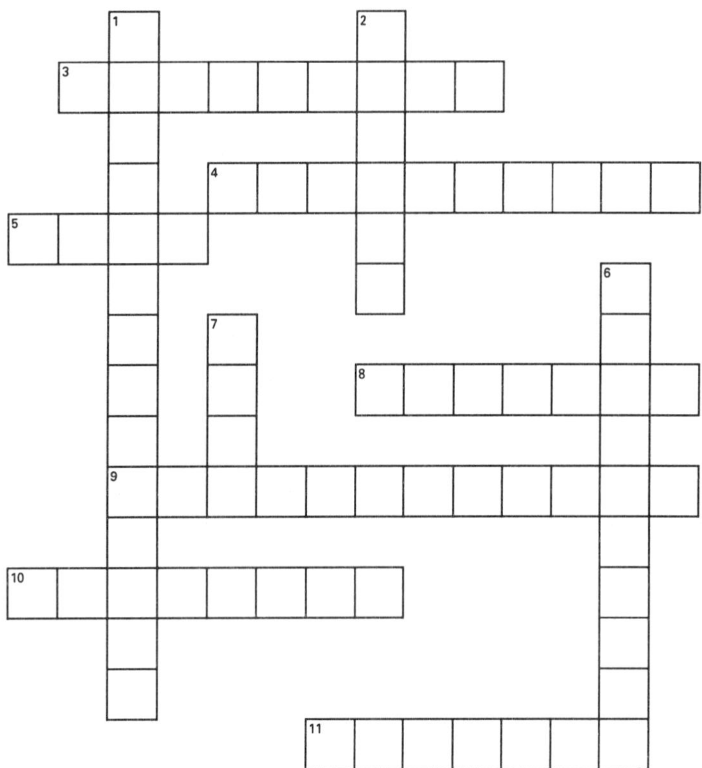

Across

3. Determined by how well you know the receiver

4. Important when sending goodwill messages

5. Commercially produced and sent in place of typed letter

8. _______________ Greetings

9. Message sent for a one-time favor

10. _______________ messages build good relationships

11. Letter used to familiarize customer with the company

Down

1. Messages sent for accomplishments

2. Approach used in goodwill messages

6. Message of sympathy

7. Request for a reply to an invitation

CASE PROBLEMS

Congratulations

1. Derek Martin was transferred to your company's branch office in Dallas, Texas, 10 years ago. Since his arrival in Dallas, he has been trying to get accepted into the Dallas Symphony. Last week he was accepted. Write a complete letter to Derek congratulating him on his accomplishment.

2. Hog Barn has been operating three restaurants in Missouri. The company has just announced an expansion of its operation to a five-state area. You are the loan officer for the Rolla State Bank. Write a letter to Darryl Gipson, president of Hog Barn, congratulating him on the expansion. Add any necessary details to make this a complete letter.

3. One of your high school classmates has been elected president of the Student Government Association at the school she attends. This position is quite prestigious since the school has over 15,000 students. Prepare a letter of congratulations for the accomplishment. Add necessary details.

Condolence

4. Green Bottle Manufacturing was hit by a tornado that destroyed its building. Fortunately, the tornado occurred at night and no one was injured. Assume that you are manager of Swain's Realty and have a vacant building that you would like to make available to Green Bottle. Write a condolence letter to Green Bottle and add information to make it a complete letter.

5. Casi, the daughter of Cyndi Gomez, a system analyst for your company, was killed yesterday in an accident involving a drunk driver. Write a letter to Mr. and Mrs. Gomez expressing your sympathy.

6. Heidi Wisehart started a small business in your community last year and was doing quite well. About three months ago the economy slowed down causing financial problems for Ms. Wisehart. Last week her business declared bankruptcy. It seems to you that the bankruptcy was caused by the economic slowdown and not by poor management on the part of Ms. Wisehart. Write her a letter of condolence adding necessary details.

Appreciation

7. You are the scoutmaster for Post 442 in Reston, Virginia. You invited Houston Nutt to give the charge (motivational speech) to the scouts at an awards ceremony. He gave an outstanding presentation. Write a letter thanking him for this act of courtesy.

8. You chaired a regional Special Olympics in your community. You would like to send a letter to each of the volunteers who made the event successful. Write a personalized form letter that could be sent. Details should be added to the letter to make it complete.

9. You have just completed serving as state president of a professional organization. You would like to send thank you letters to the individuals who served on the board of directors during your term of office. Compose a letter that would be personalized but still could be sent to everyone on the board.

Invitation

10. You are a junior partner in a local CPA firm which has recently hired two new CPAs. You and your spouse would like to have them and their guests to an informal dinner at your home. Write this invitation including necessary details such as time, date, and directions to your home.

11. The band in your school is having its annual pancake breakfast. Write a form letter that could be sent to the businesspersons in your community inviting them to this annual fund-raiser. Include all the details that the message receivers would need.

12. Your community is opening a new youth recreational center. The facility will provide activities for ages 4 through 18. Write a form letter that can be personalized and sent to all area residents inviting them to the open house.

Holiday Greeting

13. Lambert's Insurance Brokers is sponsoring a Valentine Dinner and Dance for its employees and their guests. As the human resources manager, prepare a memo that could be sent to the employees. The memo should contain an RSVP so that adequate food can be ordered.

14. Capital Investments has leased Water World, a water recreational park, for July 3. You are the human resources manager for the company. Write a memo wishing all employees a happy Fourth of July and inviting them and their families to Water World. Add any necessary details to make this a complete message.

15. The Tender Steak House would like to provide a free Thanksgiving dinner to all senior citizens in your community. It feels that the best method of inviting the senior citizens for the holiday treat is to have a letter appear in the local newspaper. Write a letter that could be printed in your local newspaper.

Welcome

16. You are the president of Panorama Shores Homeowners' association. Each month the association holds a block party for the residents of the subdivision. Write a letter welcoming new residents to the neighborhood and inviting them to attend the next block party. Add necessary details.

17. You are the president of the Student Government Association and would like to welcome all freshmen to your campus. The school administration has furnished you with a list of these individuals. Prepare a letter that could be sent to these freshman.

18. Morgan and Gunn is a large accounting firm that hires interns from colleges and universities. As personnel director for the firm, you are responsible for welcoming new employees. Write a personalized form letter to be sent to the new interns, welcoming them to the firm. Remember that the company usually hires the outstanding interns after they earn their degrees.

CHAPTER 15

Business Studies and Proposals

LEARNING ACTIVITIES

True or False?

Circle T if the statement is true; circle F if the statement is false.

T F **1.** The first task in the planning step in a business study is to define the scope of the study.

T F **2.** The Gantt chart is an effective way to show the budget for a business study.

T F **3.** Secondary sources of information include individuals, company files, and observations.

T F **4.** Primary information is published information gathered from company, public, or college libraries.

T F **5.** The least costly survey technique is the mail survey.

T F **6.** Survey questions should be developed from the factors being studied.

T F **7.** Managers should avoid using informal observation to obtain information because it is not a scientific technique.

T F **8.** To analyze data means to look at the parts by comparing and contrasting them.

T F **9.** The analysis of data should be subjective.

T F **10.** Business proposals should be viewed by writers as persuasive messages.

T F **11.** The most important, and probably the largest, section in most proposals is the benefits section.

T   F   **12.** The proposal summary section tells what parts are included in the proposal, but it should not try to tell what the content is in those parts.

T   F   **13.** When responding to an RFP, be sure to provide all information requested, even if you do not feel it is information helpful to your proposal.

T   F   **14.** A good way to present the description-of-the-solution section in a business proposal is to relate the content to each of the benefits listed earlier in the proposal.

T   F   **15.** Every proposal will have an evaluation plan.

Multiple Choice

Write the letter that represents the best answer in the blank at the left.

__________   **1.** Which of the following is the best statement of a problem for a business study?
- **a.** How can we find out the best methods for processing account payments?
- **b.** A study to process account payments more effectively.
- **c.** To determine the most effective method for processing account payments.
- **d.** To study the most effective methods to process account payments.

__________   **2.** The best way to limit the scope of a study is to
- **a.** select factors that will be studied.
- **b.** set a budget limit that will not be exceeded.
- **c.** establish a commitment to a time schedule.
- **d.** agree with your manager on a problem statement.

__________   **3.** The survey question that will yield the most comparable and useful information is the
- **a.** open-ended question.
- **b.** leading question.
- **c.** interview question.
- **d.** forced-answer question.

__________   **4.** Recommendations in a business study should follow from the
- **a.** findings.
- **b.** analysis.
- **c.** conclusions.
- **d.** benefits.

__________   **5.** Which of the following statements about business studies is the LEAST true?
- **a.** They are required infrequently in business.
- **b.** They are conducted to provide solutions.
- **c.** They are a common business activity.
- **d.** They are limited in scope.

__________ **6.** The most important proposal element among the following is the
   a. proposal summary.
   b. description of the proposed solution.
   c. problem or need.
   d. evaluation plan.

__________ **7.** The outcomes to be realized if the proposal solution is implemented are most likely to appear in what section of a proposal?
   a. Purpose
   b. Problem or need
   c. Benefits of the proposal
   d. Background

__________ **8.** The best description of business proposals from a proposal writer's viewpoint is that they are
   a. certainties.
   b. requirements.
   c. responsibilities.
   d. opportunities.

__________ **9.** Which of the following should NOT be placed in an appendix to a business proposal?
   a. Product specifications
   b. Organization's history
   c. Description of the solution
   d. Qualifications of personnel

__________ **10.** The best approach for writing a long, complex proposal is
   a. a team of writers.
   b. a team of writers with a team of readers giving feedback.
   c. an individual writer with a team of readers giving feedback.
   d. a team of writers with an individual writer providing coherence.

Matching

Write the letter of the best answer in the blank preceding the description. Some answers may be used more than once; others may not be used at all.

_______ 1. Third step in a study		**a.** appendix
_______ 2. Study boundaries		**b.** bibliography
_______ 3. Cost estimate		**c.** budget
_______ 4. Mail survey		**d.** conclusion
_______ 5. Personal interview		**e.** study solution
_______ 6. Periodical		**f.** evaluation plan
_______ 7. Leading question		**g.** glossary
_______ 8. Analysis summary		**h.** influence readers
_______ 9. Published material		**i.** high-response survey
_______ 10. Gantt chart		**j.** least costly survey
_______ 11. Request for proposal		**k.** objective
_______ 12. Recommendation		**l.** analysis
_______ 13. Cover letter or memo		**m.** primary information
_______ 14. Name of proposal, receiver, submitter, etc.		**n.** RFP
_______ 15. Lists contents		**o.** time schedule
_______ 16. Proposal in capsule form		**p.** secondary information
_______ 17. Definition of terms		**q.** limits of the study
_______ 18. Supporting materials.		**r.** proposal summary
_______ 19. Reference list		**s.** table of contents
_______ 20. Way to judge success		**t.** title page
		u. transmittal message

Completion

Complete each item by writing the necessary word or words.

1. The methods used to conduct a business study are called _______________________________.

2. A clear, accurate, written _______________________________ of a study can serve as an agreement about what is to be studied.

3. The boundaries of a study are determined by:

   a. _______________________________

   b. _______________________________

   c. _______________________________

4. In planning a study, you are most likely to need a consultant when you are _______________ _______________________________.

5. A helpful technique in searching for the published materials available on a given topic is a _______________________________.

6. The basic ways to survey people are:

   a. _______________________________

   b. _______________________________

   c. _______________________________

7. The two basic types of survey questions are _______________________________ and _______________________________.

8. The three basic ways to obtain primary information are _______________________________, _______________________________, and _______________________________.

9. In solicited proposals, the elements to be included in the proposal are often specified in the _______________________________.

10. A proposal is an analysis of a _______________________________ and a recommendation for a _______________________________.

11. Proposals initiated by an individual or an organization that are not in response to an RFP are _______________________________.

12. The two primary roles of the purpose statement in a proposal are to help the reader understand _______________________________ and _______________________________.

13. The benefits of the proposal represent the _______________________________ of the implementation of the proposed solution.

14. The evaluation plan in a proposal is a way to judge the ________________________________ achieved if the proposal were implemented.

15. Proposals are the ways that ________________________________ are conveyed to decision makers.

Review Questions

1. Name the five steps in conducting a business study.

2. Describe how to develop a clear, accurate, written statement of the problem for a study.

3. How does one analyze information?

4. Define what drawing conclusions and making recommendations mean.

5. Briefly describe the four ways proposals can be categorized.

6. List the qualities of successful proposals.

7. What are the common proposal elements?

8. What should the purpose of the proposal contain?

9. What does "the benefits of the proposal must be in you–viewpoint" mean?

10. Describe the nature of the proposal element called "the description of the proposed solution."

APPLICATION EXERCISES

1. Interview three students in your business communication class to determine what they think are the five most valuable things they have learned from your course thus far. Organize your findings so that you can analyze them. Determine the differences and the similarities and draw conclusions. List your conclusions.

2. List five factors you think appropriate to study for solving the following problem: To determine if school should be dismissed on the Tuesday of election day.

3. Analyze the following data, draw conclusions, and make a recommendation.

   Number of employees who want a flextime work schedule: 67 of 100
   Number of employees who want to come in early and leave early: 34
   Number of employees who want to work the regular schedule: 33
   Number of employees who want to come in late and work late: 33

4. Write a proposal to your instructor making a case for the final grade in your course being awarded on a pass/fail basis.

5. List the benefits that you would include in a proposal that employees and their families be provided free health insurance as a part of their fringe-benefit program.

6. Based on your experience with the service of a retail store (fast food restaurant, department store, sporting goods store, or other retail store), write a suitable proposal for improved service that could be given to the store manager.

CHAPTER 16

Report Preparation

LEARNING ACTIVITIES

True or False?

Circle T if the statement is true; circle F if the statement is false.

T   F   **1.** Policy statements should be clear, concise, complete, and written in the first person.

T   F   **2.** Progress reports provide managers with statistical information at regularly scheduled intervals.

T   F   **3.** The inverted pyramid format used for news releases begins with a summary.

T   F   **4.** Information obtained from secondary sources and used in formal reports must be footnoted, but footnoting is optional in informal reports.

T   F   **5.** Not all formal reports contain the same parts.

T   F   **6.** An executive summary of a multipage report is normally no longer than two pages.

T   F   **7.** The scope defines the boundaries of the study.

T   F   **8.** The purpose of the procedures section is to inform the reader of the methodology used in the study.

T   F   **9.** Pages in the supplementary section should be numbered by placing small roman numerals at the bottom of each page.

T   F   **10.** The appendix contains items directly related to the study but excluded from the body to improve readability.

Multiple Choice

Write the letter that represents the best answer in the blank at the left.

__________ 1. Which of the following is NOT a preliminary part of a formal report?
   a. Glossary
   b. Abstract
   c. Letter of transmittal
   d. List of illustrations

__________ 2. Which of the following is NOT a division of a formal report?
   a. Preliminary
   b. Body
   c. Appendix
   d. Supplementary

__________ 3. Which two parts may be combined in some formal reports?
   a. Letter of authorization and letter of transmittal
   b. Conclusions and recommendations
   c. Glossary and bibliography
   d. Procedures and findings

__________ 4. Which of the following is NOT true about news releases?
   a. If more than one page, *-more-* should be printed at the bottom of each page.
   b. Contact person's name and phone number should be shown on news release.
   c. It should be doubled spaced.
   d. It should contain a conclusion.

__________ 5. The report used primarily for routine reporting within an organization is the
   a. letter report.
   b. formal report.
   c. memo report.
   d. technical report.

Completion

Complete each item by writing the necessary word or words.

1. The two types of written reports are ______________________________ and
   ____________________________.

2. The cover for a written report should contain ______________________________ and
   ____________________________.

3. The ______________________________ indicates why the study was conducted.

4. Preliminary pages should be numbered using ____________________ numerals, and the
   body should be numbered with ____________________ numerals.

5. A report's _____________________ and _____________________ should be indicated in the report title.

6. Terms that are defined in a formal report should be included in a _____________________.

7. The _____________________ clearly identifies the specific situation researched.

8. A short report used to communicate routine information within an organization is a _____________________.

9. A news release should end with a _____________________ or a _____________________.

10. A technical report is used to communicate _____________________ _____________________ information.

Review Questions

1. Describe the purpose of policy statements and discuss how they are used in business organizations.

2. List and describe the body parts of a formal report.

3. List and describe the supplementary parts of a formal report.

4. Compare a progress report with a periodic report.

APPLICATION EXERCISES

1. A professional organization in your area of study has awarded you a four-year scholarship. One requirement for continuation of the scholarship is that you submit an annual report to the organization's scholarship committee giving details of the progress you have made during the past year. Write a report giving these details for the most recent year. Include in the report your educational plans for completing your degree.

2. Your local Industrial Foundation has hired you for the summer to prepare a report on the quality of the school system in your city. This report will be given to companies considering a move to your city. The report must include all levels of education in the area. Gather the facts and write a formal report that could be used to convince businesses to move to your city.

3. A student organization on your campus is initiating new members. It would like to honor the initiates by having an article appear in the local newspaper. Write a news release for the organization.

WORD PUZZLE

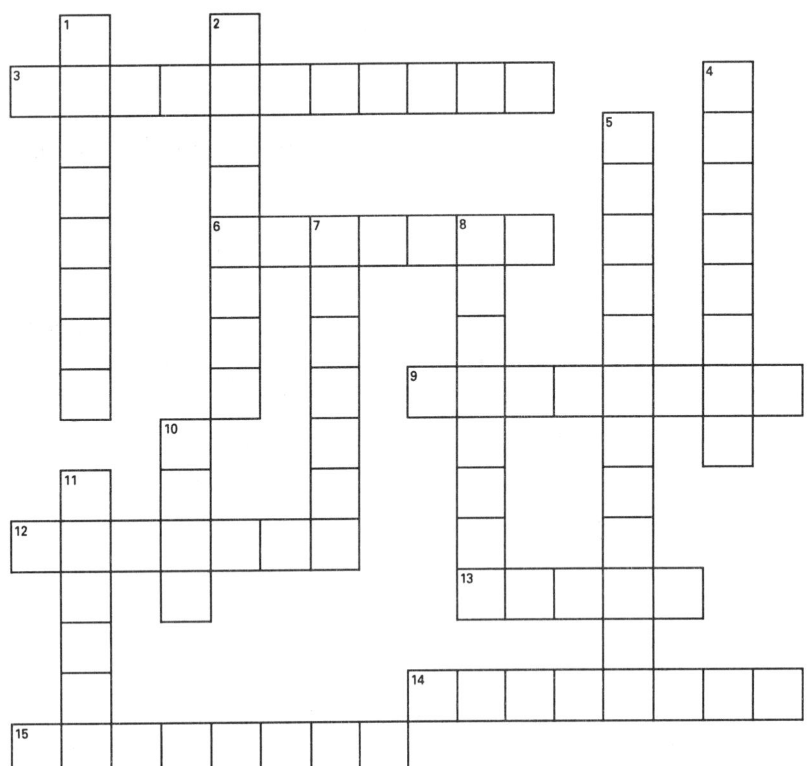

Across

3. May be combined with recommendations
6. Abstract
9. Published at regularly scheduled intervals
12. Dots in table of contents
13. Boundaries of study
14. Comparison of findings
15. Report of significant changes

Down

1. Company guidelines
2. Definitions
4. Contains indirectly related material
5. References
7. Official record of meeting
8. News _______
10. Main section of report
11. External report

CASE PROBLEMS

1. Americana Collectibles currently does not use telecommunication in its operations. As a new employee of the company, prepare a report for upper management outlining the enormous use of telecommunication equipment in businesses throughout the United States. Present the data given below in the best form to convince management that Americana needs to expand into telecommunication.

	Telecommunication Equipment	
Year	**Total Dollars Spent**	**Number of Companies Using Equipment**
1994 (est)	$1,145,800,000	12,330,175
1993	790,555,600	10,525,850
1992	420,883,793	7,190,335
1991	303,520,175	5,840,287
1990	193,645,200	4,210,495

2. Scenic Vacations is a travel agency that is expanding to provide charter trips for groups. These charter trips would be for one, two, or three days. Scenic has two options for providing these charter trips: (1) pay a flat rate for the use of buses from a bus company, or (2) purchase its own buses and hire its own drivers.

    In the first option, Scenic would pay $1.05 a mile to rent the buses from a bus company. The bus company would provide the driver and the bus.

    In option 2, Scenic would purchase a bus for $195,000 and hire its own driver. A driver can be hired for $0.34 a mile and $20 a day for meals. The driver would be provided with $50 a day for a room on overnight trips. Scenic would have an annual insurance cost of $30,000 and fuel and maintenance costs of $0.52 a mile.

    Prepare a report that could be sent to Scenic Vacations' owner, Terry Carpenter, recommending the option that should be selected. Include in the report a plan for charging groups that use the travel agency for their excursions.

3. You have been asked to speak at an Honors Seminar on gender equity in business publications. You analyze by gender the number of articles accepted for publication in professional business journals. Use the results of your investigation (shown on the next page) to prepare a report that could be presented to each participant.

Publication	Year	Number of Articles	Author	
			Male	Female
A	1993	74	67	48
	1992	72	71	59
	1991	75	62	60
	1990	65	51	47
B	1993	80	45	59
	1992	82	54	53
	1991	81	51	62
	1990	80	42	58
C	1993	68	50	63
	1992	73	59	60
	1991	70	62	54
	1990	69	65	46

CHAPTER 17

Graphic Aids

LEARNING ACTIVITIES

True or False?

Circle T if the statement is true; circle F if the statement is false.

T   F   **1.** An illustration must be placed in an appropriate location to enhance effectively the written message of the report.

T   F   **2.** Illustrations within a report should be identified by numerals or letters.

T   F   **3.** Art images saved on a diskette for later importation into a word processing document are called *clip art*.

T   F   **4.** A source note should be used whenever content for an illustration is obtained from another source.

T   F   **5.** A pie chart should never contain only one exploded segment.

T   F   **6.** A flowchart shows lines of authority among the various positions within an organization.

T   F   **7.** A line graph is a good graphic aid for illustrating changes over time.

T   F   **8.** The data being illustrated determines the interval between each vertical and horizontal line on a line graph.

T   F   **9.** When used as a graphic aid, a map should never be larger than five inches in size.

T   F   **10.** Drawings emphasize differences in statistical data.

Multiple Choice

Write the letter that represents the best answer in the blank at the left.

__________ **1.** The best graphic aid to simplify complicated written procedures is the
  a. flowchart.
  b. organization chart.
  c. line graph.
  d. pictograph.

__________ **2.** The best graphic aid to illustrate how the parts of a whole are distributed is the
  a. organization chart.
  b. pie chart.
  c. stacked bar graph.
  d. drawing.

__________ **3.** A positive–negative bar graph
  a. shows plus or minus deviations from a fixed reference point.
  b. shows changes over a period of time.
  c. shows changes in more than one value at a time.
  d. shows differences in values within variables.

__________ **4.** The most appropriate graphic aid to show trends over a period of time is the
  a. simple bar graph.
  b. line graph.
  c. map.
  d. broken-bar graph.

__________ **5.** Which of the following statements about graphic aids is NOT correct?
  a. Illustrations must be titled.
  b. A graphic aid should appear prior to the text describing it.
  c. Graphic aids should be numbered consecutively.
  d. Titles may be placed above or below the illustration.

Completion

Complete each item by writing the necessary word or words.

1. Any illustration used to assist a reader in understanding the text material is a

   ____.

2. Illustrations that indirectly relate to the written text should be placed

   ____.

3. ___________________________________ are used whenever content for an illustration is
   obtained from another source.

4. Tables are printed displays of words and numbers arranged in ____________________________
   and _________________________.

5. _________________________________ illustrate relationships among departments and personnel within the departments.

6. _________________________________ positions are connected by broken or dotted lines in an organization chart.

7. A _________________________________ chart may have a segment exploded to emphasize the segment.

8. A _________________________________ graph shows differences in values within variables.

9. The two types of line graphs are _________________________________ and _________________________________.

10. A personal touch can be added to a business report by including a _________________________________.

Review Questions

1. When and how should illustrations obtained from other sources be identified?

2. Explain why a drawing may be an effective graphic aid for illustrating a complicated idea or procedure.

3. Discuss the appropriate use for each of the five variations of bar graphs.

WORD PUZZLE

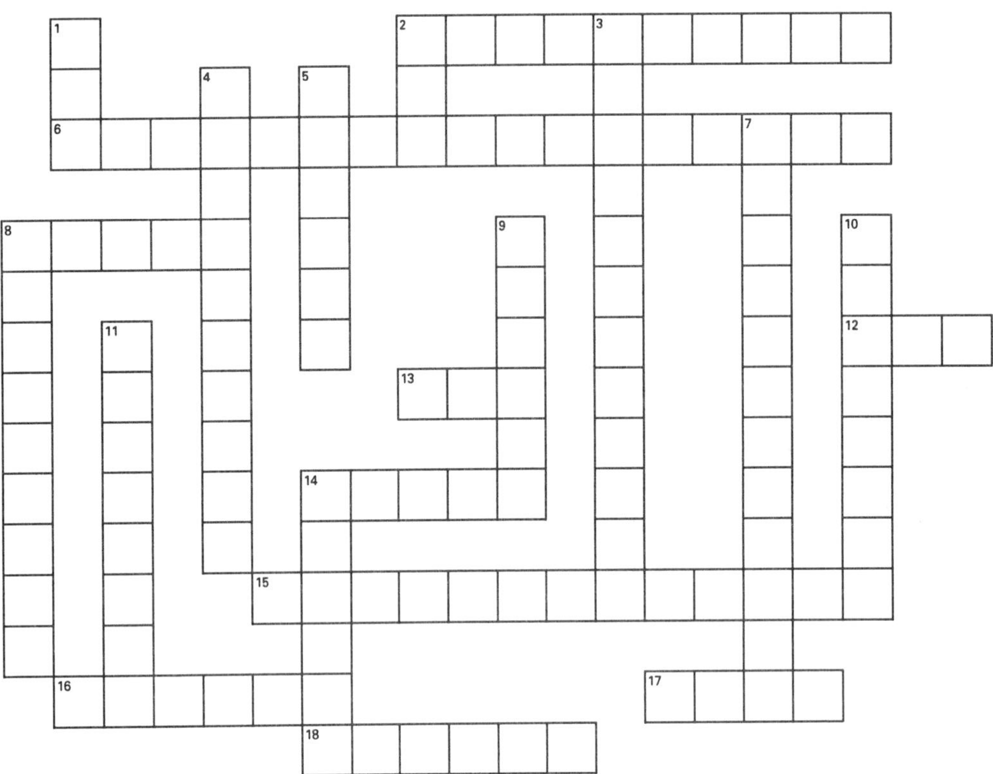

Across

2. Adds personal touch

6. Graph that shows deviations from a fixed reference point

8. Flow __________

12. Clip __________

13. Graphs that may be simple, broken, or stacked

14. Data presented in rows and columns

15. Pie chart shows __________

16. Used to identify lines in a graph

17. Graph that shows changes over a period of time

18. Line graph showing one value

Down

1. Shows geographic relationships

2. Chart showing how parts relate to one another

3. Chart showing lines of authority

4. Uses images of items

5. __________ bar graph

7. Graphic aid

8. Direction in which pieces of pie chart are displayed

9. __________ note

10. Omit clutter and emphasize desired details

11. Line graph showing changes in more than one value at a time

14. Line graphs illustrate __________

APPLICATION EXERCISES

1. Construct the most appropriate graphic aid to show the comparison of sales to expenses for Classic Boots in the past five years.

Year	Sales	Expenses
1990	$432,300	$274,000
1991	415,000	261,300
1992	633,700	315,250
1993	595,500	310,760
1994	903,100	429,875

2. The following data show how a student could spend his or her day. Construct a graphic aid that most effectively illustrates how each activity compares with the other activities.

In class	3 hr 30 min
Studying	4 hr 15 min
Eating	1 hr 45 min
Resting	6 hr 45 min
Entertainment	3 hr 45 min
Working	4 hr 0 min

3. Teri's Auto Supply conducted sales throughout the year at different percentage reductions. Records were kept to correlate the percentage of sales discount with the total amount of sales. Using the following figures, construct a graphic aid that illustrates the comparisons most effectively.

Amount of Reduction	Amount of Sales
10%	$ 8,450
20%	15,100
30%	19,300
40%	23,250
50%	25,775
60%	13,425

4. Benton School keeps records of its sports-related injuries that require medical attention. Construct a graphic aid that best illustrates the number of injuries within individual sports for each of the past five years.

Year	Basketball	Football	Soccer	Track
1994	1	19	0	3
1993	2	26	1	1
1992	2	20	0	4
1991	3	31	2	2
1990	1	27	1	1

5. Estimate your personal expenses for a period of one month. Use a graphic aid to illustrate the distribution of the expenses.

CHAPTER 18

Listening and Nonverbal Messages

LEARNING ACTIVITIES

True or False?

Circle T if the statement is true; circle F if the statement is false.

T   F   **1.** Stimuli are assigned meanings through a person's mental filters.

T   F   **2.** People normally can hear at a faster rate than they can speak.

T   F   **3.** A speaker's message should be evaluated after he or she has completed the entire presentation.

T   F   **4.** A speaker may volunteer more information if you give negative feedback.

T   F   **5.** A speaker may change the meaning of an oral message by displaying facial expressions.

T   F   **6.** Forming a rebuttal to the material presented will help you concentrate on the speaker's presentation.

T   F   **7.** Since the distance between communicators affects the communication, it should not vary.

T   F   **8.** For a salesperson to show confidence in his or her product, the salesperson should squeeze the customer's hand as tightly as possible during a handshake.

T   F   **9.** Nonverbal communication may transmit an unintentional message.

T   F   **10.** Nonverbal messages are always present in oral and written communication.

Multiple Choice

Write the letter that represents the best answer in the blank at the left.

__________ 1. Which is NOT a mode commonly used to listen to messages?
   a. Cautious listening
   b. Careful listening
   c. Skimming
   d. Scanning

__________ 2. Which of the following best describes scanning?
   a. This mode is used to remember all details of the message.
   b. This mode is the least demanding of all three modes.
   c. The listener concentrates only on selected material of specific interest to him or her.
   d. This mode is used to remember the general concept of an oral message.

__________ 3. Which of the following is NOT an effective guideline for listening?
   a. Keep an open mind.
   b. Use feedback.
   c. Maximize notetaking.
   d. Stop talking.

__________ 4. Which of the following is NOT a speech characteristic that may be a barrier to listening?
   a. Tone
   b. Unusual pronunciation
   c. Volume
   d. Dialect

__________ 5. Which of the following is NOT true about nonverbal communication?
   a. May make a first impression on a receiver.
   b. Creates images that will be easy for the sender to change.
   c. Occurs in both written and oral communication.
   d. Is always present.

Completion

Complete each item by writing the necessary word or words.

1. The listening process consists of the following:

   a. ____

   b. ____

   c. ____

   d. ____

2. The three modes of listening are ________________________________,
   ________________________________, and ________________________________.

3. The ________________________________ mode is the least careful type of listening.

4. Daydreaming is a ________________________________ distraction.

5. Dialects, jargon, unusual pronunciations, and speech impairments are
   ________________________________ barriers.

6. One of the best ways of gaining information is through effective ________________________________
   ________________________________.

7. Types of nonverbal communication are:

   a. ________________________________

   b. ________________________________

   c. ________________________________

   d. ________________________________

8. Manner of dress communicates a ________________________________ message.

9. A type of nonverbal communication that depends on the proximity to the person in charge is
   ________________________________.

10. Smiles and frowns are forms of ________________________________ language.

Review Questions

1. Describe the differences between hearing and listening.

2. Why is it important for a good listener to know the purpose of the message?

3. How can effective listening improve your communication?

4. Describe several forms of body language and explain how each transmits a nonverbal message.

APPLICATION EXERCISES

1. Observe how space is allocated on your campus. Include office and parking spaces. Write a
   short report analyzing your observations.

2. Analyze a local, state, or national figure according to speech characteristics and nonverbal communication. Be prepared to demonstrate these nonverbal actions to see if the class can guess
   who is being portrayed.

3. Observe young children, young adults, and elderly adults at a common gathering. Record the nonverbal messages that each group presents. Describe the messages that are transmitted.

4. Record the nonverbal messages that several instructors in your school transmit. Bring the list, without the instructors' names, to class and discuss with the class the meanings associated with each message. Do any of the meanings distract from the instructors' presentations?

WORD PUZZLE

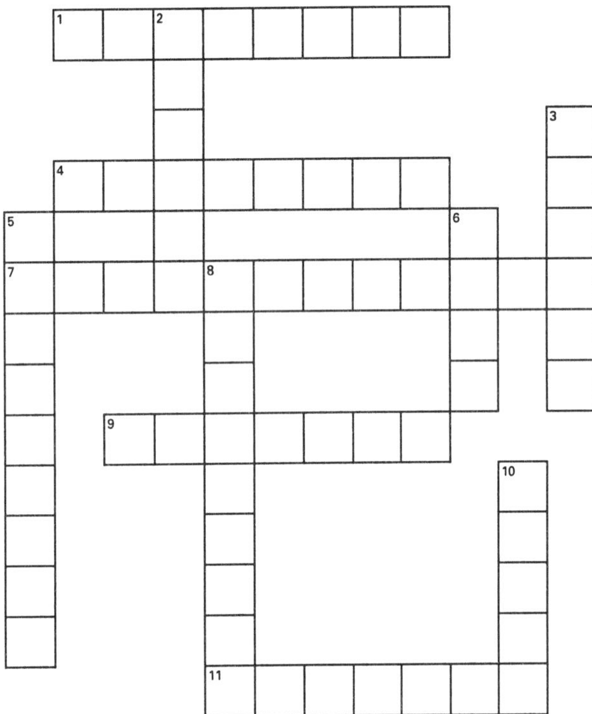

Across

1. Least careful mode of listening

4. Mode of listening for general concepts

7. Assigning meaning to stimuli

9. Stimulation of auditory nerves by sound waves

11. Form of body language

Down

2. Listening is an __________ process

3. A speech characteristic barrier

5. Eliminates unwanted stimuli

6. A type of nonverbal communication

8. Remembering at a later time

10. Includes the size of a physical area

CHAPTER 19

Oral Communication Essentials

LEARNING ACTIVITIES

True or False?

Circle T if the statement is true; circle F if the statement is false.

T   F   **1.** A business that provides products and services needed by customers meets all the requirements for success.

T   F   **2.** Lower-level managers spend more time in oral communication than do higher-level managers.

T   F   **3.** Written communication ability is more critical to effective leadership than is oral communication ability.

T   F   **4.** A speaker can relax his or her sound-producing organs with two or three deep breaths.

T   F   **5.** It is possible to indicate comparisons and contrasts with voice pitch.

T   F   **6.** While voice pitch can be used effectively for emphasis, voice volume refers simply to being heard by others.

T   F   **7.** It is important to talk slower in one-to-one communication than it is in one-to-large group communication.

T   F   **8.** The way in which you join sounds is called *enunciation.*

T   F   **9.** Charisma refers to personal magnetism and grace that causes others to react positively and favorably toward the person possessing this quality.

T   F   **10.** Having unrealistic expectations for your oral communication can cause a lack of self-confidence.

Multiple Choice

Write the letter that represents the best answer in the blank at the left.

__________ 1. The most extensive oral communication is required of employees in
   a. purchasing.
   b. computer operations.
   c. unions.
   d. marketing.

__________ 2. Pitch refers to the
   a. volume of your voice.
   b. timbre of your voice.
   c. highness or lowness of your voice.
   d. strength of your voice.

__________ 3. To avoid a monotone voice, you should vary your
   a. pitch, volume, and speed.
   b. pitch and volume.
   c. volume and speed.
   d. pitch and speed.

__________ 4. If you exhibit too little confidence when speaking to others, they will
   a. reject you.
   b. feel discomfort.
   c. feel negative toward you.
   d. reject your message.

__________ 5. A good way to gain confidence when speaking to a group is to
   a. keep the emphasis on the listeners and use the you–viewpoint.
   b. visualize your audience as sitting there in their underwear.
   c. tell yourself that you can do it.
   d. concentrate on yourself and how you sound.

__________ 6. The best way to be sincere is to
   a. be persuasive.
   b. avoid humor.
   c. project a congenial appearance.
   d. believe in what you are saying.

__________ 7. To have comfortable eye contact with a group audience, you should try to look
   a. slightly above the heads of the group members.
   b. into the eyes of every member of the group.
   c. into the eyes of selected members of the group.
   d. at the foreheads of the group members.

__________ **8.** Gestures should be
      a. carefully designed.
      b. contrived.
      c. natural.
      d. repetitious.

__________ **9.** True feelings are best communicated by
      a. eye contact.
      b. facial expressions.
      c. words.
      d. posture.

__________ **10.** The correct volume level during an oral presentation is loud enough
      a. to convey strength.
      b. for your average listener to hear you.
      c. to be heard by interested listeners.
      d. for every one in your audience to hear you.

Completion

Complete each item by writing the necessary word or words.

1. Your oral communication effectiveness will depend on the ________________________________ of your voice and the ________________________________ of your presence.

2. Supervisors, managers, and executives are required by their positions to give ________________________________ through their oral communication.

3. The three major categories of oral communication are:

    a. ________________________________

    b. ________________________________

    c. ________________________________

4. When you try to inhale deeply in preparation for speaking, the air should go all the way to the ________________________________.

5. Pitch refers to the ________________________ or ________________________ of the voice.

6. Comparisons, contrasts, finality, doubt, or hesitation can be shown by the ________________________________.

7. The important point in regard to the rate of speed you use while you speak is to ________________________________ your rate.

8. Too little or too much confidence are both caused by ________________________________.

9. The over-confident speaker projects a know-it-all attitude and a
____ for the audience.

10. You can project enthusiasm and feel enthusiastic if you speak with energy and
____.

Matching

Write the letter of the best answer in the blank preceding the description. Some answers may be used more than once; others may not be used at all.

__________ 1. Business success depends on	**a.**	air
__________ 2. A type of oral communication	**b.**	appearance
__________ 3. Raw material for speaking	**c.**	communication
__________ 4. Personal magnetism	**d.**	enthusiasm
__________ 5. Voice volume	**e.**	facial expression
__________ 6. Too much confidence	**f.**	tone
__________ 7. Excite an audience with	**g.**	must be sufficient to be heard
__________ 8. Gain credibility with	**h.**	know-it-all attitude
__________ 9. Conveys true feelings	**i.**	one-to-large group
__________ 10. Way message sounds	**j.**	charisma
	k.	sincerity

Review Questions

1. To be successful as a leader, your oral communication ability must include what capabilities?

2. Discuss the managerial uses of oral communication in business.

3. Name some employee positions that use oral communication extensively.

4. Indicate the two major improvements you can make in your oral communication ability.

5. How do you avoid the "troublesome *t*'s"?

6. Explain how you find your natural pitch.

7. What are good ways of determining that you are speaking loudly enough?

8. What are the appropriate speeds of speaking (a) for large groups, and (b) for one-to-one conversations and small groups?

9. How do you stress selected parts of oral messages with the speed of speaking?

10. What is the role of facial expressions in oral communication?

11. Discuss the appropriate role of gestures in oral communication.

12. Why is posture important in oral communication?

13. Describe how a speaker can develop an effective level of confidence.

14. Discuss the importance of an oral communicator showing enthusiasm, sincerity, and friendliness.

15. What does "strengthen your presence with a good personal appearance" mean?

WORD PUZZLE

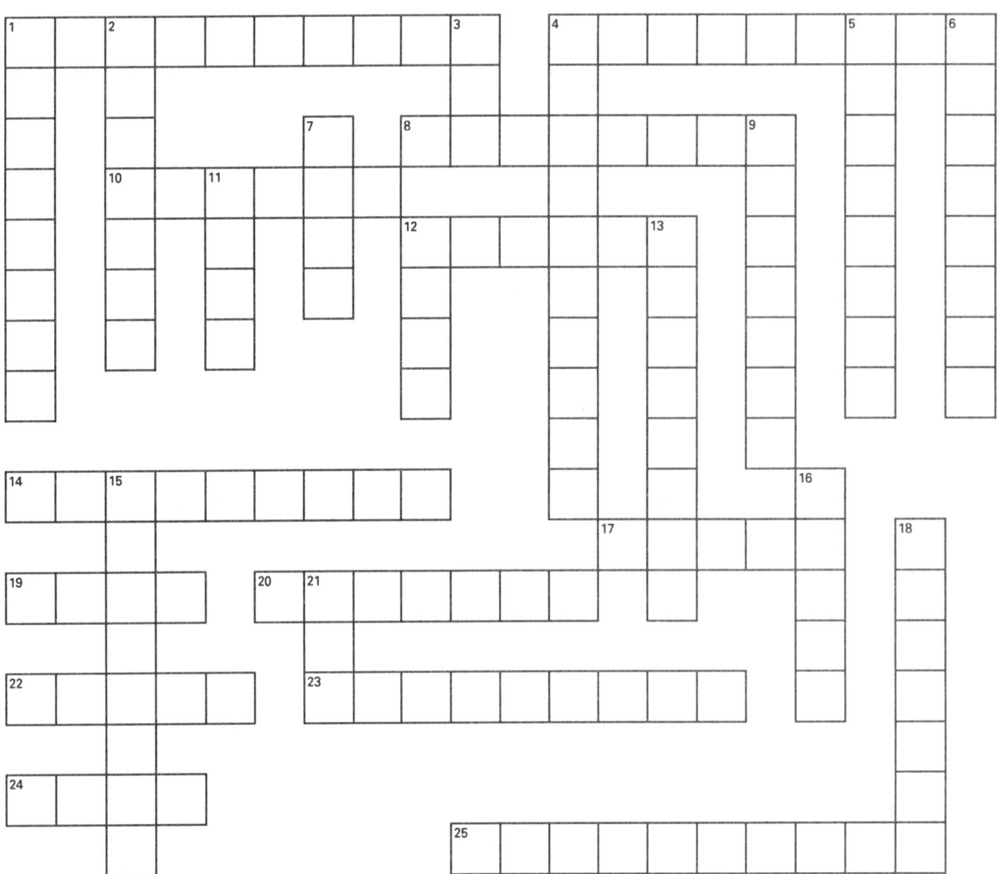

Across

1. Self-________
4. A leader
8. Nonverbal signals
10. Communication flow to those above you
12. Needed to be heard
14. Body part important in proper breathing
17. Can be high or low
19. Useful for nonverbal communication
20. Should not be rigid
22. Vary this, depending on group size
23. Sound out parts
24. Communicates true feelings
25. Must fit the audience and occasion

Down

1. Personal magnetism
2. Not contrived, but ________
3. Important contact
4. It's contagious
5. Inside
6. Outside
7. Opposite of written
9. Opposite of failure
11. Part of a sentence
12. Same as change
13. Used to stress ideas
15. Group of people
16. Communication instrument
18. Believable
21. ________-to-small group communication

CHAPTER 20

Oral Communication Applications

LEARNING ACTIVITIES

True or False?

Circle T if the statement is true; circle F if the statement is false.

T   F   **1.** Oral communication situations are more complex than written communication situations.

T   F   **2.** Important human variables in oral communication include the formality of the situation, the location, and the purpose of the communication.

T   F   **3.** The real messages in interpersonal oral communication are the nonverbal behaviors of the senders and receivers.

T   F   **4.** The desired amount of eye contact varies from culture to culture.

T   F   **5.** We have a distorted perception of time while holding a phone and waiting for someone to speak to us.

T   F   **6.** The first item of business at each meeting of a small group should be the determination of a meeting agenda.

T   F   **7.** In resolving group conflicts, an option the leader should NOT use is to simply move on to the next agenda item after deciding the conflict is not worthy of the group's time.

T   F   **8.** It is each participant's responsibility in a small group meeting to encourage appropriate participation by all members of the group.

T   F   **9.** An extemporaneous oral presentation is one that has to be given without preparation.

T   F   **10.** For a large-group oral presentation, you should analyze the knowledge, interests, opinions, and emotional state of the members of the audience.

T   F   **11.** Because interpersonal oral communication has to be simpler than written communication, it is not as vital to analyze your receivers when giving a speech as it is when writing a letter or memo.

T   F   **12.** A good visual aid for a large-group oral presentation is a copy of the speech being given.

T   F   **13.** The overall organizational framework you should use for an oral presentation is (1) opening, (2) body, and (3) closing.

T   F   **14.** Most practiced and professional speakers are nervous before speaking to an audience.

T   F   **15.** A question-and-answer session following an oral presentation can be used effectively to enhance the speaker's relationship with the audience.

Multiple Choice

Write the letter that represents the best answer in the blank at the left.

__________   **1.** Most critical business decisions are made through
    a. one-to-one oral communication.
    b. one-to-small group oral communication.
    c. one-to-large group oral communication.
    d. written communication.

__________   **2.** The best guide for face-to-face communication is to be
    a. appropriately disagreeable.
    b. appropriately aggressive.
    c. appropriately assertive.
    d. appropriately angry.

__________   **3.** Which of the following is NOT a good way to avoid telephone tag?
    a. Ask for best time to call back.
    b. Leave a message indicating when you are available.
    c. Call at regular intervals.
    d. Leave a message indicating the purpose of your call.

__________   **4.** The quality of thinking that emerges from small-group meetings is usually
    a. lower than one person can achieve alone.
    b. higher than one person can achieve alone.
    c. the same as one person can achieve alone.
    d. has no relationship to what one person can achieve alone.

_________ **5.** Which of the following techniques is NOT helpful when trying to resolve group conflicts?
  a. Postpone the discussion to give time for reflection.
  b. Reflect the group feeling of frustration by being firm.
  c. Take a group vote.
  d. Seek a compromise through group discussion.

_________ **6.** In a small-group discussion, which of the following is NOT an appropriate way to control a participant who talks too much?
  a. Stress to the whole group that everyone should have an opportunity to speak.
  b. Suggest that the group is covering the same territory again and needs to move on.
  c. At the end of a sentence, thank the excessive talker and ask others to comment.
  d. Remind the group that when one person talks too much it is unfair to the other members.

_________ **7.** A large group oral presentation given from brief notes is called
  a. extemporaneous.
  b. impromptu.
  c. memorized.
  d. manuscript.

_________ **8.** What organizational plan would be best for an oral presentation in which a person is being introduced to an audience?
  a. Time sequence
  b. Problem–solution
  c. Cause–effect
  d. Direct or indirect

_________ **9.** Which of the following visual aids would best support an oral presentation in which a new product is being introduced?
  a. Handouts explaining the product
  b. Transparency picture of the product
  c. Model of the product
  d. Audio tape describing the product

_________ **10.** Which of the following visual aids would best promote audience interaction in exploring alternatives?
  a. Poster
  b. Overhead transparency
  c. Computer-generated visual
  d. Movie

Matching

Write the letter of the best answer in the blank preceding the description. Each answer may be used only one time.

__________ 1. Environmental variable

__________ 2. Appropriate eye contact with southeast Asians

__________ 3. Size of small groups

__________ 4. Small-group meetings

__________ 5. Read to audience

__________ 6. No preparation time

__________ 7. Given from notes

__________ 8. Responsible for success

__________ 9. Nonverbal behavior

__________ 10. Oral communication

a. 3 to 20

b. manuscript speech

c. are costly

d. is dynamic

e. impromptu speech

f. real message

g. timing

h. extemporaneous speech

i. 10 percent of the time

j. small group leader

k. over 20

Completion

Complete each item by writing the necessary word or words.

1. In interpersonal oral communication, three important human variables are:

    a. ____

    b. ____

    c. ____

2. Five important keys for successful face-to-face oral communication are:

    a. ____

    b. ____

    c. ____

    d. ____

    e. ____

3. The purpose of carefully observing nonverbal behavior in oral communication is to receive the

    ____.

4. Telephone tag is ____
   ____.

5. Committees formed in businesses are usually one of two types:

   a. ____

   b. ____

6. The first task in conflict resolution is to be sure
   ____
   ____.

7. The primary purpose of large-group oral presentations is ________________________
   or ____.

8. The three major parts of a large-group oral presentation are:

   a. ____

   b. ____

   c. ____

9. The speech-delivery technique recommended to you in this chapter is
   ____.

10. Some speech authorities recommend that you rehearse your presentation aloud and while on
    your feet at least ________________________ times.

Review Questions

1. Describe the dynamics of an interpersonal oral communication situation.

2. Describe how you can be considerate of your caller when using the telephone.

3. Discuss the types and sizes of small groups.

4. What are the keys for successful small-group leadership?

5. What are your responsibilities as a small-group participant?

6. Explain why the extemporaneous oral presentation is the most effective delivery style.

7. Describe the variety of audiovisual aids you might select for use in an oral presentation.

8. What are the keys for successfully delivering an oral presentation?

9. Describe how to handle stage fright during the delivery of an oral presentation.

10. Explain how you "end positively" when you are delivering an oral presentation.

APPLICATION EXERCISES

1. Observe two 30-minute segments of the network news (ABC, CBS, CNN, or NBC) and record any errors in speaking that you noted.

2. Record all the problems you have in telephone conversations over a 48-hour period.

3. Write a report on what you have noted are the attributes of :

    a. poor small-group leaders

    b. good small-group leaders

    c. poor small-group participants

    d. good small-group participants.

4. Analyze the large-group oral communication skills of a selected public figure in your state.

CHAPTER 21

The Job Search and Resume

LEARNING ACTIVITIES

True or False?

Circle T if the statement is true; circle F if the statement is false.

T　F　**1.** The first step in a job campaign is to find positions for which you can apply.

T　F　**2.** Solicited positions are positions that are available but are unlisted or unadvertised.

T　F　**3.** The most valuable source of information about jobs will likely be your school or college placement office.

T　F　**4.** One of the common services of college placement offices is the maintenance of credentials files for candidates.

T　F　**5.** Newspaper advertisements are a good source of information only about jobs in a given geographical area.

T　F　**6.** Either the employee or the employer will have to pay the private employment agency a significant fee for its services.

T　F　**7.** State governments provide employment services.

T　F　**8.** Since you are the product you are selling in your job search, you will want your resume to contain only positive information.

T　F　**9.** In analyzing your qualifications, the most important facts to list are evidences of your accomplishments.

T　F　**10.** A personalized resume is less powerful than a general resume.

T   F   **11.** Most employers prefer the functional resume format over the reverse chronological resume format.

T   F   **12.** The education section should always follow the resume opening.

T   F   **13.** If your high school record is fairly recent and shows considerable accomplishment, include it in your resume; otherwise, omit it.

T   F   **14.** Because employers want to know, be sure to list your grade-point average even if it is not at the A or B level.

T   F   **15.** You are encouraged to provide full information on your references, including their business telephone numbers.

Multiple Choice

Write the letter that represents the best answer in the blank at the left.

__________ **1.** Which of the following employment services does NOT provide information about jobs in the private sector?
- **a.** College placement office
- **b.** State government employment office
- **c.** Federal government employment office
- **d.** Private employment agency

__________ **2.** Parallelism in a resume means
- **a.** starting all material at the left margin.
- **b.** using the same part of speech to start a series of items.
- **c.** having complete sentences for the narrative resume content.
- **d.** giving the same amount of space to each section.

__________ **3.** Most employers prefer the
- **a.** personalized, reverse chronological resume.
- **b.** personalized, functional resume.
- **c.** general, reverse chronological resume.
- **d.** general, functional resume.

__________ **4.** The best arrangement for a resume for a college graduate who has extensive experience is
- **a.** opening, references, education, references.
- **b.** opening, education, experience, references.
- **c.** opening, experience, education, references.
- **d.** opening, experience, references, education.

__________ **5.** The primary purpose of a resume is to
  a. summarize information about you.
  b. prepare you for completing an application form.
  c. communicate clearly your strengths and weaknesses.
  d. obtain a job interview.

__________ **6.** The purpose of the summary of qualifications is to
  a. enable managers to determine if you match their openings.
  b. indicate your personal job or career goals.
  c. detail your strengths.
  d. summarize the opening data in your resume.

__________ **7.** Which of the following parts of an Education section in a resume is the most important?
  a. Courses
  b. Organization memberships
  c. Achievements
  d. Dates of attendance

__________ **8.** Which of the following is the general recommendation on including reference data in a resume?
  a. Do not provide reference data.
  b. Provide complete reference data.
  c. Indicate references are available on request.
  d. Indicate references are on file in college placement office.

__________ **9.** The maximum number of pages for a resume is
  a. one.
  b. two.
  c. three.
  d. the number needed to cover essential information.

__________ **10.** Employment laws
  a. prohibit a job applicant from revealing his or her gender.
  b. permit a job applicant to reveal his or her race.
  c. permit an employer to ask for the name of an applicant's religion.
  d. prohibit an employer from asking for the name of an applicant's college.

Matching

Write the letter of the best answer in the blank preceding the description. Some answers may be used more than once; others may not be used at all.

__________	**1.** Advertised or listed positions	**a.** unsolicited positions
__________	**2.** Listing of qualifications	**b.** personal information
__________	**3.** Optional section	**c.** reverse chronological resume
__________	**4.** Presents information by skills/knowledge	**d.** placement office
		e. interviewer
__________	**5.** Unadvertised positions	**f.** solicited positions
__________	**6.** Job information source	**g.** obtain job interview
__________	**7.** Resume purpose	**h.** accomplishments
__________	**8.** Presents most recent information first	**i.** resume
__________	**9.** Nontraditional resume	**j.** reference
__________	**10.** Critical resume content	**k.** functional resume

Completion

Complete each item by writing the necessary word or words.

1. Your most important business communication will be about your ____.

2. The most helpful publication available at a college placement office is the ____.

3. Two major services of many college placement offices are ____ and ____.

4. The primary purpose of private employment agencies is to ____.

5. State government employment agencies list employment opportunities both ____.

6. In your job campaign, ________________________________ are the product you are selling.

7. In analyzing your qualifications, four helpful categories are:

    a. ____

    b. ____

    c. ____

    d. ____

8. The primary purpose of a resume, along with an application letter, is
    ____.

9. Name the two basic types of resumes: (a) ____
    and (b) ____.

10. Name the two basic formats of resumes: (a) ____
    and (b) ____.

WORD PUZZLE

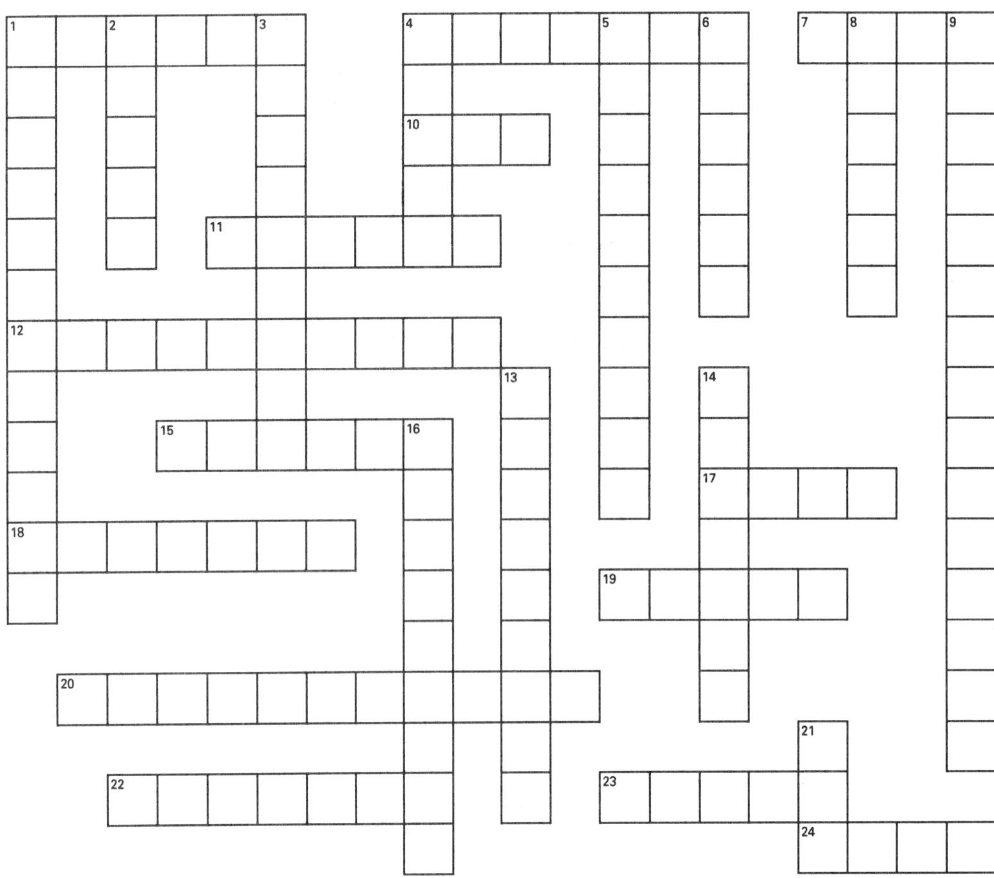

Across

1. Summary of qualifications
4. Not personalized
7. Personal ________ sheet
10. Source of jobs
11. ________ objective
12. Work
15. Type of achievement
17. Synonymous with resume
18. Special abilities
19. Minimum number of references
20. Unadvertised
22. ________ employment agency
23. Don't include with resume
24. Paper color for resume

Down

1. Job ________
2. A special capability
3. Training
4. ________ point average
5. Should be favorable
6. Solicited jobs are
8. Evidences of achievements
9. Achievements, learning, contributions
13. Unpaid employment
14. Not chronological order
16. Advertised
21. Position

CHAPTER 22

Employment Communication and Interviewing

LEARNING ACTIVITIES

True or False?

Circle T if the statement is true; circle F if the statement is false.

T   F   **1.** Application letters are sales letters—with you as the product.

T   F   **2.** You can combine a personalized resume and a general application letter.

T   F   **3.** The primary purpose of an application letter is to get the job.

T   F   **4.** You can be quite creative in the attention-getting opening of an application letter.

T   F   **5.** You should indicate how you meet the employer's job requirements in an application letter.

T   F   **6.** All application letters try to motivate the employer to act.

T   F   **7.** The most important part of an application letter is the section in which the writer tries to convince the employer that he or she fits the job.

T   F   **8.** As an interviewee, you should have some key questions of your own for the interviewer.

T   F   **9.** When asked in an interview what salary you would expect, the best answer is, "I am open on the salary question."

T   F   **10.** The amount of appropriate eye contact with interviewers is 25 percent of the time, and possibly less depending on their cultural backgrounds.

T   F   **11.** In accepting an interview invitation, suggest how busy you are by indicating it is somewhat difficult for you to schedule a time for the interview.

T   F   **12.** Even if you are definitely not interested in the job, it is still appropriate to follow up an interview.

T   F   **13.** If you think it has been too long since you have heard about your application with an employer, it is appropriate to call or write.

T   F   **14.** It is best to let your current employer know, if you can, that you have a job search underway.

T   F   **15.** When resigning from a job, you should use the direct plan of communicating.

Multiple Choice

Write the letter that represents the best answer in the blank at the left.

__________ **1.** An application letter should be written following the guidelines for
    a. neutral messages.
    b. persuasive messages.
    c. goodwill messages.
    d. negative messages.

__________ **2.** The most important part of an application letter is the
    a. attention-getting opening.
    b. summary of qualifications.
    c. action-promoting close.
    d. logical explanation.

__________ **3.** An application letter is your opportunity to
    a. show how you fit the job.
    b. impress the reader with your communication ability.
    c. transmit your acceptance of a job interview.
    d. convince the reader that he or she should give you the job.

__________ **4.** In the close of an application letter, the way to get an interview is to
    a. plead for it.
    b. ask directly for it.
    c. imply that you want it.
    d. not push it.

__________ **5.** If you have a number of appointments and commitments during the next few weeks, in the close of an application letter discussing a possible interview time you should
    a. mention that your schedule is not completely free.
    b. briefly and generally list your major appointments and commitments.
    c. say that hopefully your schedules will match.
    d. offer to be at the interviewer's office at his or her convenience.

__________ **6.** For most employers, the final decision on whether to offer a job will be based on the
  a. application letter.
  b. resume.
  c. interview.
  d. follow-up communication.

__________ **7.** Your preparation to interview begins
  a. when you start a job campaign.
  b. after the analysis of your qualifications.
  c. after you have prepared your resume.
  d. when an interview invitation is received.

__________ **8.** If you are asked during an interview, "Do you consider yourself ambitious?" the best response is
  a. Yes.
  b. No.
  c. Yes. I think my responsibility to myself, to my future family, and to my employer is for me to be ambitious.
  d. No. Too much ambition can cause people to sometimes make the wrong decisions for themselves and their company.

__________ **9.** Appropriate behavior during an interview does NOT include
  a. being assertive.
  b. being vague.
  c. being calm.
  d. talking positively about other employers.

__________ **10.** Following up an interview
  a. is inappropriate.
  b. should be done with a phone call.
  c. should be done with a letter.
  d. should be done in person.

Completion

Complete each item by writing the necessary word or words.

1. The three major parts of a well-designed application letter are:

   a. ____

   b. ____

   c. ____

2. In the opening of an application letter, the two most important things to do are:

   a. ____

   b. ____

3. The three most important things to do in the middle section of an application letter are:

   a. ____

   b. ____

   c. ____

4. In the close of an application letter, the candidate should:

   a. ____

   b. ____

   c. ____

5. In preparation for an interview, you should prepare yourself to answer the question, "What salary do you expect in this job?" Two good sources of information about salaries being paid for similar jobs are ____ and ____.

6. The signals an interviewer may give you that an interview is ending are ____.

7. If an interviewer challenges you by asking difficult questions or by appearing disinterested or even irritated, you should ____.

8. After an interview, the candidate should ____.

9. Following up a pending application may be ____.

10. When you have accepted an employment offer and have completed a successful job campaign, it is important to ____.

APPLICATION EXERCISES

1. Write the first sentence of an application letter for a job as an advertising copy writer for a public relations firm.

2. Write the last sentence for an application letter in which you are seeking an interview.

3. What answer would you give in an interview to a first question similar to the following: "Why should we hire you for this position?"

4. Write the sentence in a resignation letter in which you give your employer the specific news that you are resigning.

5. Write the last sentence in a letter accepting a new position.

6. You have been offered two managerial positions by comparable companies. You have decided to accept the offer from the company that pays more and that is located closer to your family. How would you phrase the key rejection part of the letter in which you turn down the other company's offer?

7. Write the first sentence in a thank-you letter you are sending to the four persons who agreed to serve as your references in your recent successful job campaign.

WORD PUZZLE

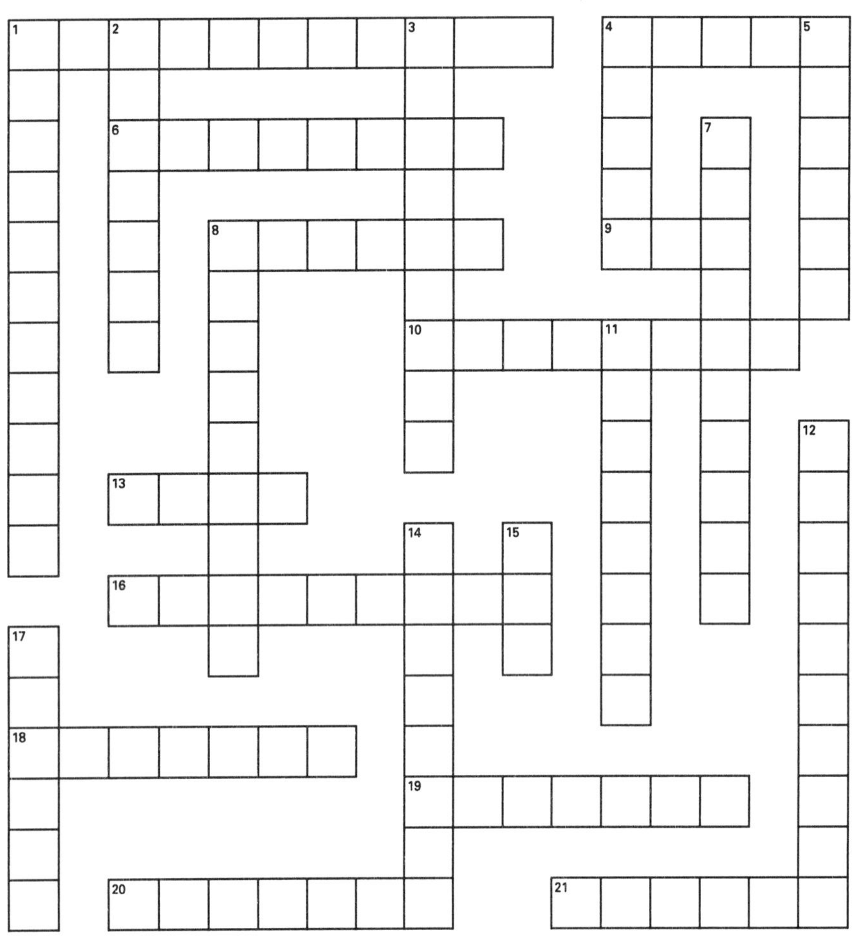

Across

1. Request for employment
4. _________ confidence
6. Check quality of interview
8. Job worth
9. Your qualifications should _________ the job requirements
10. Not direct
13. _________ attention in opening
16. Be ready to answer _________
18. Abstract of qualifications
19. Include for reference
20. Create
21. Quit

Down

1. Ask _________ questions
2. _________ for an interview
3. Meeting with potential employer
4. Length of application letter
5. Opposite of indirect
7. Plan ahead
8. Advertised
11. _________ the company
12. Request to come to an interview
14. Purpose of application letter is to _________ employer to read resume
15. _________ directly for interview
17. Application letter and _________ are the application packet